THE
ONLINE
INVESTOR'S
COMPANION

THE
ONLINE
INVESTOR'S
COMPANION

50 ESSENTIAL
Financial Web Sites

ROB CARRICK

John Wiley & Sons

John Wiley & Sons Canada Ltd
22 Worcester Road
Etobicoke, Ontario
M9W 1L1

National Library of Canada Cataloguing in Publication Data

Carrick, Rob, 1962-
    The online investor's companion : 50 essential financial web sites

ISBN 0-470-83159-6
    1. Electronic trading of securities—Computer network resources. I. Title.
HG4515.95.C38 2002   332.63'2'02854678   C2002-903305-2

Production Credits
Text and Cover Design: Interrobang Graphic Design Inc.
Printer: Tri-Graphic Printing

Printed in Canada
10 9 8 7 6 5 4 3 2 1

To my family: Theresa, Will, and Jamie.
Thanks for all your help and understanding.

Contents

Introduction

First, let me come clean with you. My name is Rob Carrick and I'm an Internet investing addict. I check my stocks online at least once or twice a day and at any given moment, it's more than likely that I know exactly what the markets are doing. I browse investing sites often to look for investing ideas and commentary, and I sometimes dissect a stock online just for the hell of it. No, the Internet hasn't turned me into a millionaire or an investing prophet. But I will say this: Thanks to the Internet, I'm firmly in control of my investing destiny and supremely confident I'll get where I'm going.

What about you? Just the fact that you're reading this book suggests that you understand what a phenomenal resource the Internet represents to investors. If you're still unclear about this, imagine that you've experienced the joy of reading for the first time and you find out there's such a thing as a library. It's no exaggeration to suggest that the Internet is as much of a revelation to someone who is interested in investing. The Internet is truly a repository of information on every subject in the world, but it excels in investing and personal finance. The Net's capability to bring fresh, up-to-the-minute information to you at any time of day is uniquely suited to the fast-moving nature of the financial markets. Radio and television simply can't give you what the Internet can.

Let's quickly look at the kinds of financial information you can find on financial Web sites (Web sites, for those who are unsure, are like information rest stops on the cyberhighway called the Internet). In the area of personal finance, you'll find that the Web permits a degree of comparison shopping that was impossible in the pre-Internet era. Financial Web sites can help you compare mortgage rates at many different institutions, help you shop for insurance, and give you tax tips. More impressive are the investing resources you'll find online.

Online investing at its most basic is getting a stock quote or update on the stock markets during the trading day. From there, you can create an online stock or mutual fund portfolio. You can track investments you actually own, or those that you might want to buy sometime in the future. What else? If you were researching a particular stock, you might do some graphing to check its performance over the past year, then call up a company profile. To probe further, you might look at some research produced by analysts whose job it is to bore down into a company and report back on how solid the foundation is. Financial columnists may also have pronounced on this company—the Internet will document this. Financial news services may have covered this company—the Internet will give you all of this as well.

Maybe now you're ready for some specialized online investing services. There's a Web site mentioned in this book that will give you a good idea of how risky a company's stock is (RiskGrades), while another site will give you some indication about whether the stock is hot or cold right now (Stockscores). Then there are the sites that allow you to swap questions and answers with other investors interested in the same stock—the so-called online message boards. Mutual funds are covered just as thoroughly on the Internet.

Who's the Typical Online Investor?

If there's one thing I've learned about online investing, it's that there's no generalizing about who's doing it. Teenagers and university students are active online investors, blue-collar workers and executives are doing it, and seniors are doing it as well. And forget about gender breakdowns; I've heard from as many women in all of these categories as men.

You might think that online investing is synonymous with self-investing, or handling your affairs without the help of a broker or other kind of investment adviser. This is only partially true. While the Internet is the backbone of any do-it-yourselfer's investment strategy, it's also an invaluable tool for people who have an adviser. Using the Web, you can generate ideas to discuss with your adviser, and you can double-check recommendations your adviser gives you.

The Web is also for people who want to learn about investing and aren't yet ready to put their money to work. Read avidly on the Web and you'll soon qualify for a Ph.D. in investing. ■

I shouldn't oversell the Internet, because it has its problems. Frankly, there's way too much information out there. You can waste astounding amounts of time mucking around on second-rate Web sites looking for information that's displayed with crisp precision elsewhere. In fact, whatever you would like to find out about a stock or mutual fund can often be found on five or more different Web sites. The purpose of this book is to guide you to the best online investing resources. If you're just starting out, this is your roadmap. If you're already an online investor, this is where you learn about the shortcuts and tricks that can take you where you want to go faster and more informatively. One certainty about online investing: No matter how many great resources you know about, there are others to discover.

It's a safe bet that some new investing Web sites appeared during the period between when this book was written and when it appeared in bookstores. That's the Internet, always improving and renewing itself (check the book's End Note for tips on assessing new financial Web sites). Likewise, it's conceivable that a site mentioned in this book will be defunct or radically changed when you read this. The Internet is competitive, demanding of innovation and unforgiving to those who fall behind. It's also a brutally tough business environment. One thing for certain is that all the sites mentioned in this book are leaders in one way or another. For example, Yahoo Finance is ahead of the rest in delivering all-around Swiss-army-knife usefulness, while Globeinvestor.com is the absolute best at providing a seamless database on both Canadian and U.S. stocks, and Morningstar.ca is nirvana for those who want mutual fund research.

Some of the material in this book started out in a weekly Web site review I wrote for *The Globe and Mail*, the newspaper where I work as a personal finance columnist. One day, the *Globe's* investing editor, Michael Den Tandt, suggested I collect the reviews into a book. Here they are, greatly expanded and updated.

HOW TO USE THIS BOOK

You'll notice that each of the 50 essential Web sites is assigned a pair of ratings, one for overall usefulness and one for Canadian content. Consider the usefulness rating an indication of how indispensable a site is. A site with five stars fulfills its purpose brilliantly and is probably one you'll use often. Sites with lesser usefulness ratings are still essential resources, but ones that have a narrower purpose and are thus not going to be as beneficial to you. A site with a one-star usefulness rating will be helpful on rare occasions, but when you do need it you'll find it quite worthwhile. The Canadian content rating was developed in response to the preponderance of U.S. content on the Internet. It's intended to help you tell at a glance whether a site has anything to offer if you're researching Canadian stocks and mutual funds.

Now let's take a quick look at how Web sites were chosen for the book. Here are my three main criteria:

Utility: Above all, a site has to be authentically useful, and not just provide a novelty service. Most of the sites in the book provide a package of useful services, but there are a few that do one thing only, though they do it very well. It's my hope that you'll try some of the sites in this book and wonder how you got by without them.

Presentation and Ease of Use: Some Web sites in this book are beautiful to behold, and some are butt ugly. Nice aesthetics are sometimes a good indicator that significant resources have been poured into a site. But as long as a site is cleanly laid out and presents its services in an accessible manner, I'm happy. You'll notice as you read through this book that I haven't made too many specific criticisms about design or layout. The reason is that any critique I offer of a Web site's layout might be irrelevant because of a redesign by the time you read this.

Distinctiveness: The services offered on every Web site in this book stand out in one way or another. It could be for providing quality stock research reports or stock-screening tools, or for a clever blending of many features found elsewhere on a piecemeal basis.

Specifically excluded from consideration for this book were Web sites operated as billboards for investing newsletters, sites used to sell proprietary stock-picking strategies, and sites operated by brokers, banks, mutual fund companies, or financial advisery firms.

It's Only My Opinion...

I've tried to be thorough and scientific about selecting Web sites for this book, but at the end of the day I recognize that the whole exercise is pretty darn subjective. I happen to think Yahoo Finance is a great investing Web site, and I think it scores well in each of the three criteria listed above. Still, others may think it's a dull-looking agglomeration of services you can find elsewhere. Everyone's got an opinion, and everyone's right in his or her own way. If you disagree violently with any of my choices or, more important, if you want to point out a great site for my consideration, send an e-mail to robcarrick@hotmail.com. ∎

The presentation in this book has been designed to give you a quick profile of a site, as well as an in-depth discussion that describes the best features. At the top of the section for each Web site you'll find the usefulness and Canadian content ratings, as well as a brief description of the appeal of each site and a note on whether its services are free (virtually all have at least some free services). While reading about the sites in this book, you'll notice that some words are contained within quotation marks. The idea here is to help you locate the features I'm discussing when you visit the actual Web site. For example, when I talk about the "Investing" section of MSN Money, you can count on the fact that there's an "Investing" button to click on that will take you directly to this part of the site.

You'll notice that there are no Web site screen shots in this book. The reason is that Web sites change their design fairly frequently and before long the screen shots would be out of date. Redesigns may also change some of the features described in this book, and relocate some of the navigational buttons I mention. If this is the case, I apologize for the inconvenience.

At the end of each section is an "At a Glance" recap that you can use if you just want a quick overview of a site. Finally, there's a "Links" area that suggests similar Web sites that are worth checking out. I'd love you to read this book cover to cover, but lots of people will want to jump around randomly or simply browse. However you read the book, I hope you find it useful. Happy surfing.

Getting Started

All you need to get going is some very basic equipment: A computer with an Internet connection and a Web browser, either Microsoft Internet Explorer or Netscape Navigator. If you don't have a computer at home, maybe you can use one at work (on your lunch break, of course), or one at a library or an Internet café. The price of personal computers is dropping so fast that you might be surprised at how cheaply you can acquire a system.

The specifications of the computer you use don't matter that much as long as you have a reasonably up-to-date machine at your disposal (I wouldn't bother wheeling out that old Commodore 64 in your basement). Much more important is the speed of your Internet connection. The faster your connection, the more you'll enjoy online investing. In fact, it's more important to have fast Internet access for online investing than for almost any other Internet application. The reason is that many financial Web sites are loaded with numbers, words, and graphics. Even with a fast Internet connection, these Web pages can take a while to load on your computer. With a slow connection, you're bound to hit a wall of frustration sooner or later.

So what exactly do you need in terms of an Internet connection? I'm inclined to say that a 56.6K modem is the bare minimum, although there's nothing to stop you from using a 36.6K or slower modem if that's all you have. When I started using Internet investing sites, it was part of my job as personal finance columnist at *The Globe and Mail*. Our office had high-speed Internet access, which I always enjoyed having because it made Web pages quick to download and, by nature, I'm somewhat impatient. Then I came home one day and checked out an investing Web site there using our 56.6K modem. Agony. Not too long afterwards, we got high-speed Internet access at home.

Essential Software

Beyond the Web browser, there's one product that is essential and another that's optional but highly recommended. The essential software program is an **Adobe Acrobat Reader**, which allows you to download documents of one to one hundred or more pages and then print any or all pages. You'll quickly see the benefit of this free program if you visit the Multex Investor Web site (this site is one of the essential 50) and want to download a stock research report. Without an Acrobat Reader, there's no way you could do this. If a Web site requires you to have an Adobe Acrobat Reader to download documents, chances are good it also has a link to the Adobe Web site, where you can easily download the Acrobat Reader for free. If not, just head to www.adobe.com.

A highly recommended software program, also free, is **RealPlayer** from the company Real.com. Visit the InvestorCanada Web site (also one of the essential 50) and you'll understand why RealPlayer is so useful. This Web site conducts interviews with mutual fund managers, economists, and other investing professionals and then archives them on the site. People with RealPlayer can listen to these programs at their convenience simply by clicking on a link that automatically summons the RealPlayer and gets it ready to play. If a Web site requires RealPlayer, chances are it offers a link to the Real.com Web site at www.real.com. Watch out—there is a free RealPlayer and a deluxe version that will cost you money. ∎

On the topic of Web browsers, it doesn't really matter whether you go with Netscape or Microsoft as long as you have a reasonably recent version. You'll know you need an upgrade if you continually have problems getting Web pages to load properly. Here's where to go for free upgrades of your browser software:

- For Netscape Navigator: www.netscape.com (Note: There have been reports of problems being experienced by people using Netscape Navigator 6, which was the latest version at press time)

- For Microsoft Internet Explorer: www.microsoft.com/windows/ ie/default.htm

Along with an Internet-connected computer, you'll find it useful to have a printer. When I find some interesting reading material on the Web, I often print it and then read it on the bus home from work, or in the evening.

A Note about Web Addresses

The full and proper format for a Web address, or URL (stands for universal resource locator), is http://www.sitename.com or, in the case of some Canadian sites, http://sitename.ca. Now that we've got that straight, let's shorten things. From here on in, all Web sites in this book will leave out the http:// part.

One other thing. While most Web addresses have a www (for World Wide Web) in them, a few such as Yahoo Finance and MSN Money, do not. Don't be thrown when you see the URLs for these sites written without a www in front, as in finance.yahoo.com or moneycentral.msn.com.

Now that we've got the basics out of the way, let's get down to business.

EIGHT GREAT THINGS TO DO ON FINANCIAL WEB SITES

1. Stock Quotes

I think the last time I used a newspaper to get a stock quote was 1996. These days, I just can't imagine having to wait until the next morning to find out how a stock did during a day's trading. People do still use the newspaper to keep up with their stocks, and I see why as long as they don't have an Internet-connected computer at work or at home. If you are able to go online, though, you can keep up with your stocks daily, hourly, or more often if you like.

It can safely be said that every financial Web site in creation offers stock quotes, and that many non-financial sites do as well. If you want a quote for a Canadian stock, it's easiest to stick with Canadian Web sites. Many U.S. sites offer quotes for Canadian stocks, but there's usually a prefix or suffix you have to add to the stock symbol to make the quote server understand you're talking about a Canadian stock. If you don't type a Canadian symbol in correctly, you'll run into trouble. For example, you might want a quote for Telus Corp. on the Toronto Stock Exchange. Type Telus's symbol - T - into a U.S. quote server and you'll get AT&T.

Canadian Quotes on U.S. Sites

There's often a trick for prying Canadian stock data out of U.S. sites. For example, Yahoo Finance requires you to type .TO after a stock, as in BCE.TO. BigCharts, CBS MarketWatch, and MSN Money require you to type CA: in front of the symbol, as in CA:BMO. Some other sites require T. in front of the symbol, as in T.CP.

Your last resort if you can't figure out how to get Canadian data out of a U.S. site is to check the site's "help" section. ∎

The vast majority of quotes you'll come across on the Internet will actually tell you what a stock or stock market was doing 15 or 20 minutes ago. These are called delayed quotes, as opposed to real-time quotes, which represent the latest price or index level. There are a few free sources of real-time quotes (keep reading for more details), but generally they're only available to clients of online brokers, or through deluxe subscription packages offered by financial Web sites. How do delayed quotes work? Here's the Globeinvestor.com Web site's explanation (this is typical of other sites):

> "During trading hours (weekdays, 9:30 a.m. to 4 p.m.), price quotes are delayed 15 minutes for securities that trade on Canadian Exchanges and Nasdaq and 20 minutes for securities that trade on the New York Stock Exchange and AMEX. End-of-day prices and market data are typically published on the site 15 to 20 minutes after the markets close."

Delayed quotes are useful for those times when you're mildly curious about what a stock is doing, or if you simply want to check in on a stock in your portfolio. When you're trading stocks online, you'll want the up-to-the-moment information conveyed by a real-time quote. Beyond real-time quotes are streaming quotes, which update automatically and continuously on your computer screen. Streaming quotes are even more of a premium service than real-time quotes.

Just so you know, newspapers will carry stock tables for the foreseeable future, but they're waiting eagerly for the day when enough people are connected to the Internet that they can drop this space-clogging coverage.

tip: A good Web site for trying online stock quotes for the first time: Globeinvestor.com at www.globeinvestor.com.

Free Real-Time Quotes

Some Web sites make you pay for real-time quotes, but there are a few that offer freebies. Here are a few examples:

- **FreeRealTime.com** (www.freerealtime.com): Sign up for a free membership on this site and you get real-time quotes as part of a very good collection of stock research tools. Finding the real-time quotes is as simple as typing a stock symbol in the ticker box in the upper left corner of the homepage and then clicking on the "Go" button.

    The actual quotes are more detailed than you'll usually get from an online broker. In addition to bid and ask prices (the most investors are offering or accepting for a stock), there's also information on bid and ask size. Sizing tells you how many board lots (100 shares) of a stock are available at the bid and ask prices. Also included in the quotes are the tick trend for the stock, which shows whether the preceding trades were up or down, and the size of the average trade that day.

- **ThomsonFN** (www.thomsonfn.com): Register for this free service and you have the option of getting your quotes in real time or with a delay of 20 minutes. ThomsonFN's real-time quotes are less detailed than FreeRealTime.com, but they do include sizing.

- **MSN Money** (moneycentral.msn.com): Microsoft's personal finance and investing Web site offers real-time quotes as part of its suite of stock research tools. These quotes aren't the most detailed you'll find, but they're still a welcome bonus on this excellent site.

NOTE: All three of these sites offer quotes for Canadian companies listed on U.S. exchanges, but not for those listed on the Toronto Stock Exchange.

Using Free Real-Time Quote Sites: First, you'll have to sign up by providing personal information that includes your name, plus mailing and e-mail addresses. Then, you'll have to complete a couple of long and abstruse online forms in which you basically agree not to hold issuing stock exchanges liable for incorrect information, and not to distribute the data to third parties.

    The forms are the work of the New York Stock Exchange and Nasdaq, which sell real-time data to market data companies. The bottom line is that exchanges are simply trying to protect their revenue by ensuring you're not passing the quotes along or using them professionally.

The value of real-time quotes over delayed quotes is particularly obvious when the markets are flying. Even in the span of 15 or 20 minutes, stocks can take surprising twists and turns. On one occasion, I got a delayed quote from ThomsonFN at 10:46 a.m. showing C-MAC Industries up $2.74 (U.S.), or 10.96 per cent, to $27.72 on the New York Stock Exchange. Seconds later, a real-time quote showed C-MAC had surged in the interim and was actually up $3.82, or 15.28 per cent, to $28.82.

Even tamer stocks can move significantly in the span of 15 or 20 minutes. In one particular instance, a delayed quote for Royal Bank on the NYSE showed the stock was down 30 cents, or 1.03 per cent, while a real-time quote delivered moments later showed the stock had turned around and was actually up 21 cents, or .72 per cent. ■

2. Portfolio Tracking

Some of the most useless objects in all the world are the monthly statements mailed out by brokerage firms and mutual fund companies. Just what you need—a sheet of paper telling you how your portfolio was doing 10 days ago. With an online portfolio tracker, you can keep track of how your portfolio is doing at any given moment, day or night.

Portfolio trackers are not as ubiquitous as stock quotes on investing Web sites, but this may soon change. In fact, trackers are now one of the features with which Web sites compete most vigorously. Several of the more prominent investing Web sites have made it a point of pride to offer innovative trackers that use incredible graphics to show how your holdings are doing, or that offer significantly more detail than a mere monthly statement can show.

Some portfolio trackers on the Web allow you to track both U.S. and Canadian stocks, but many do U.S. stocks only. In a few cases, you can track Canadian mutual funds as well. Unless I specific otherwise, you should expect to find only U.S. stocks included in a portfolio tracker.

Before you can use a Web site's tracker, you'll usually have to sign up for the service by picking a username and password. You then follow the instructions for adding the stocks or funds that you want to track. If you want to view your portfolio, you may have to type your username and password each time. Some sites will offer you the option of remembering these secret codes so that you're instantly logged in whenever you call up the site. Avoid this option if your computer is used by others and you don't want them stumbling upon your stock portfolio while using the Web.

Portfolio trackers are great for following the stocks and funds you own, but they're just as useful for watching securities that you may want to buy in the future. Many trackers let you follow several different portfolios—you could use one to track your registered retirement savings plan and then add others for your spouse's RRSP and your unregistered account. Finally, you could add a watchlist for stocks you want to buy when they reach a certain price level.

For stocks you actually own, you'll want to add the number of shares you bought, the date you bought them, the price you paid, and, possibly, the commission you paid. That way, the portfolio tracker can keep track of exactly how much you're up or down for each stock, and for the entire portfolio. Simply monitoring the value of your holdings is a fairly basic function for portfolio trackers. Some of the more high-powered ones will produce graphs to illustrate how you're doing, while others will tell you if the companies in your portfolio have been in the news that day, or whether analysts have mentioned them in some way. As well, company names in your portfolio may be linked to information pages on the stock.

tip: A good Web site to try online portfolio tracking: SmartMoney.com at www.smartmoney.com.

3. Basic Stock Research

When I hear about an interesting stock, the first thing I like to do is find out what line of business the company is in. Then maybe I'll get a quote showing the current price, 52-week high and low, dividend yield, and price-earnings ratio. Also, I usually like to have a chart showing what the share price has done over the past year. From there, I might look at the company's financials—is this firm making money and, if so, how much have its earnings increased in recent years? I might also look at some financial ratios to gauge the company's health and profitability. All of this is basic stock research that can easily be done with a good financial Web site or two.

tip: A good Web site to do basic stock research: MSN Money at moneycentral.msn.com.

4. Consulting Stock Research by Analysts

More and more stock analysis is available on the Internet, often for free. There are two kinds of research, which we'll call unbiased and brokerage. Unbiased research is done by independent analysts who have no personal stake in a company, nor do their firms. All they do is assess companies. Brokerage research, which is always branded with the name of the brokerage house involved, is somewhat different in that it's conducted by analysts working for investment dealers that may have business relationships with the same companies being covered by the analysts. Can an analyst be objective about a company who pays her firm big bucks for advisery services and underwriting? Many investing professionals believe the answer is often no, which is why so many new sources of unbiased research are springing up.

On the Internet, there's a huge variety of both unbiased and brokerage research. Many sites offer an overview of the ratings and earnings estimates that analysts have on particular stocks. A so-called consensus rating will average out all the "strong buy," "buy," "hold," "sell," and "strong sell" recommendations and come up with a single rating. Likewise, the various earnings estimates are averaged out into a single estimate. It's also possible to download free research reports on the Web, or to download reports on a pay-as-you-go basis.

tip: A good Web site for looking up analyst recommendations and estimates: Yahoo Finance at finance.yahoo.com.
For free and pay-as-you go research: Multex Investor at www.multexinvestor.com

5. Researching Mutual Funds

Funds lack the glamour of stock, so don't expect to see coverage of them played up on any of the big investing Web sites. This isn't a problem because there are several excellent sites devoted entirely to funds. Have a fund in mind for your registered retirement savings plan? These sites will give you a detailed profile of the fund, including Top 10 holdings and recent and long-term returns. Want to buy a fund, but you don't have a clue which one? These sites have search engines, or filters, that let you sift through hundreds or even thousands of funds to find those that meet specific criteria— maybe Canadian equity funds that have returned an average 10 per cent annually for the past 15 years.

tip: A good Web site for discovering online mutual fund research: Morningstar.ca at www.morningstar.ca.

6. Screening for Stocks

Stock screens are just glorified search engines that are tuned to sift through the world of stocks to find just the ones you're looking for. Maybe you would like to create a list of financial stocks with dividend yields above 2.5 per cent, or all stocks on the TSE 300 that are up 10 per cent in the past week. To make things slightly more complex, you could specify that the financial stocks have a price-earnings ratio below 12, and that the TSE 300 stocks have a market capitalization above $100 million. There are stock screens out there that will let you set a dozen or more criteria for finding stocks. If you have a very specific idea of what you want, these screens can be an extremely effective tool. Note that some Web sites have pre-set screens that are designed for a specific purpose, say to sniff out value stocks, or high-growth stocks, or fallen stocks with turnaround prospects. In each case, the designers have loaded in a set of criteria that they believe will produce stocks of a specific type.

tip: A good Web site for trying online stock screening: Quicken.com at www.quicken.com.

Making Life Easier for Online Investors

Here are a couple of features that some financial Web sites employ to help users enjoy and share the material on the site.

Printing Web Pages: Much as we all love the Internet, we must recognize its limitations. Notably, you cannot read an investing Web site on the bus, in bed, or in the john. Unfortunately, we often find ourselves with time to read when we're in these locales. To get around this problem, why not print Web stories that catch your eye and read them later. Most investing Web sites expect you to do this, and in fact they encourage it. That's why they often have a button saying something like "print this story." Click on this button and you'll jump to a different Web page or even a new browser window where the story has been reconfigured to make it print more easily. Often, the printable version has chopped off the extraneous graphics to give you just the written material. You can always try printing any old Web page, but you may find that parts of the page are missing.

E-mailing Articles to Friends: Right beside the "print this article" button you'll often find another one inviting you to e-mail the article to a friend. You can imagine why investing Web sites encourage this sort of thing. Maybe your friend will read the e-mail and become a regular visitor. It's worth pointing out that you can e-mail Web pages yourself. If you use Netscape Navigator, just right click your mouse and select the "send page" option. With Microsoft Internet Explorer, select "file" from the menu at the top of the page, then select "send" and then "page by e-mail." ∎

7. Message Boards

Ever thought you would like to compare notes on a stock or an investing issue with other investors, in the hope that they know something you don't? If so, you'll want to try the many message boards, also called online discussion forums, available on the Internet. Think of these forums as heated conversations carried out via e-mail. Often, someone will start a thread with a provocative question, like maybe: "Is Nortel Networks poised for a surge higher?" On a good message board, investors will hash out this question in dozens and sometimes hundreds of postings. Participating in these forums can be fun, but there's no reason you can't just be a spectator who watches the proceedings.

Message boards are a big attraction on investing Web sites, which is why most big sites offer this service. If you want to get the broadest possible range of views, though, you'll go to a site that specializes in online stock talk, like Silicon Investor. Canadian stocks sometimes come up on these sites, but you may also want to try StockHouse Canada's well-used BullBoards if you're interested in domestic stocks.

Now for the downside of message boards. As careful and sceptical as you have to be when reading general investing advice on the Internet (and anywhere else for that matter), you have to be doubly cautious when reading message boards. Bluntly speaking, message boards can be sanctuaries for liars, scammers, and con artists. Some will try to talk up worthless penny stocks in which they have an interest, others will try to sabotage an unsuspecting company's stock for no apparent reason, and others are just trolling for gullible fools. Beware. For more information, see Chapter Two.

tip: A good Web site for trying online discussion groups:
Silicon Investor at www.siliconinvestor.com.

8. Educating Yourself about Investing

I've written a column on personal finance for several years, and before that I spent more than a decade as a reporter covering the investing world, economics, and business. Despite this experience, I still need help now and again understanding the odd bit of financial jargon. I have a few books on my shelf to help in these cases, but I almost always end up using the Internet because of the variety of resources out there. There are financial sites that focus on education and others that have made a point of weaving educational content into their regular services. Say you wanted to learn more about technical analysis, which involves trying to map out where stocks are going based on their current and recent trading patterns. Technical analysis is dauntingly complex, but ClearStation and Stockscores make it all seem easy. Likewise, InvestinginBonds.com will help you explore the sometimes arcane world of bonds, while Globefund.com can guide you through mutual funds.

tip: A good Web site for learning about investing:
Investopedia at www.investopedia.com.

PRIVACY AND SECURITY ISSUES

Personally, I'm indifferent to the possibility that a nefarious hacker out there in cyberspace might be able to view the stocks I track in an online portfolio. I think I'm in the minority, though. Every time I've written about online portfolio tracking, I've received numerous e-mails from readers asking about privacy. The common thread in these inquiries is that people don't like the idea of someone looking into their personal business. Fair enough, then. Let's take a close look at the privacy issues related to online investing.

Cookies

This innocuous-sounding term refers to the tiny bits of information that many commercial Web sites implant in your computer after you've visited for the first time. Every time you visit after that, your Web browser sends information back to the site announcing your arrival and providing information about you. This information might consist of all the links you've clicked on in previous sessions on that site, or products that you've purchased on the site, or preferences you've expressed about the kinds of information you want to see on the site.

Unless you set your browser to alert you every time a Web site installs a cookie on your computer, you'll be oblivious to the whole process (Warning: Cookie alerts can make Web surfing painfully slow). If you're curious about which sites have put cookies on your computer, try doing a search of your computer's hard drive for files that will generally be called cookies, or cookies.txt or Magic-Cookie. I remember the first time I checked the cookies on my computer at home. I was shocked at the number and variety of sites listed, and a little uneasy at the idea that they were all tracking my online habits in one way or another. I'd read about how privacy advocates had criticized cookies as a means for Web sites to gain access to information that they could sell or distribute to sources I knew nothing about.

After a minute or so, I got over it. Cookies are simply a necessary evil for active Internet users, especially those who use financial Web sites. I say this because financial Web sites often offer customized services, be they personalized online stock portfolios or homepages that include information selected by you, the user. It's cookies that make this all possible.

There are a couple more points about cookies that are worth noting. First, cookies aren't dangerous to your computer and they cannot be used to access your hard drive. Second, you can delete cookies with no alarming effects. Just be sure to close your browser first, or you'll find that the cookies may regenerate themselves. You can also set your browser to reject cookies outright.

Providing Personal Information to a Web Site

Many investing Web sites ask you to sign up before you can use some of their services. In doing so, you will invariably be asked to provide personal information of one sort or another, possibly your name, age, home city, mailing address, e-mail address. Financial Web sites also seem to like asking about occupation, income bracket and, in a few cases, stock-trading habits. If you have any reservations about doing this, check the site's privacy policy. Reputable sites will include a privacy policy link somewhere on their homepage, often in the fine print near the bottom.

A Sample Privacy Policy: Yahoo Finance

What this Privacy Policy Covers

- This Privacy Policy covers Yahoo's treatment of personally identifiable information that Yahoo! collects when you are on the Yahoo! site, and when you use Yahoo's services. This policy also covers Yahoo's treatment of any personally identifiable information that Yahoo's business partners share with Yahoo!.

- This policy does not apply to the practices of companies that Yahoo! does not own or control, or to people that Yahoo! does not employ or manage. In addition, this policy does not apply to Yahoo! NetRoadshow, which has its own privacy policy.

Information Collection and Use

- Yahoo! collects personally identifiable information when you register for a Yahoo! account, when you use certain Yahoo! products or services, when you visit Yahoo! pages, and when you enter promotions or sweep-stakes. Yahoo! may also receive personally identifiable information from our business partners.
- When you register with Yahoo!, we ask for your name, email address, birth date, gender, zip code, occupation, industry, and personal inter-ests. Once you register with Yahoo! and sign in to our services, you are not anonymous to us.
- Yahoo! also automatically receives and records information on our server logs from your browser including your IP address, Yahoo! cookie information and the page you requested.
- Yahoo! uses information for three general purposes: to customize the advertising and content you see, to fulfill your requests for certain prod-ucts and services, and to contact you about specials and new products.

Information Sharing and Disclosure

- Yahoo! will not sell or rent your personally identifiable information to anyone.
- Yahoo! may send personally identifiable information about you to other companies or people when:
- We have your consent to share the information;
- We need to share your information to provide the product or service you have requested;
- We need to send the information to companies who work on behalf of Yahoo! to provide a product or service to you. (Unless we tell you dif-ferently, these companies do not have any right to use the personally identifiable information we provide to them beyond what is necessary to assist us);
- We respond to subpoenas, court orders or legal process; or

cont'd

- We find that your actions on our web sites violate the Yahoo! Terms of Service, the Yahoo! GeoCities Terms of Service, or any of our usage guidelines for specific products or services.

Cookies

- Yahoo! may set and access Yahoo! cookies on your computer.
- Yahoo! allows other companies that are presenting advertisements on some of our pages to set and access their cookies on your computer. Other companies' use of their cookies is subject to their own privacy policies, not this one. Advertisers or other companies do not have access to Yahoo's cookies.
- Yahoo! uses web beacons to access our cookies within our network of web sites and in connection with Yahoo! products and services. (reprinted with the permission of Yahoo) ■

Investing Web sites that offer subscription services will generally give you the opportunity to pay by credit card. As with any online shopping site, you indicate which card you want to use, then type in the credit card number and expiration date. Exercise extreme caution about providing credit card information to a financial Web site, just as you would to any other type of site. Ensure the site is reputable, and that the service you're buying is verifiable. Also, check to see what security measures the site uses to protect the privacy of credit card data. If you're not comfortable with any aspect of an online transaction, don't do it.

Online Stock Portfolios

With many investing Webs sites, your online portfolio or portfolios will be displayed every time you go to the site's homepage. If anyone other than you uses your computer, it's conceivable that he or she could check out your bookmarks, head to an investing Web site and get a detailed look at what stocks you own, what you paid for them, and how much money you've made or lost. Even if you've just created a watch portfolio, where you follow stocks you don't own, someone could sit down at your computer and see what you've been up to. Do you really want someone to say, Hmm, I didn't know Jane was into technology stocks? Like I said a moment ago, this sort of thing doesn't worry me, but it does seem to trouble other people I've come across.

Some investing Web sites require users to submit a username and password before an online portfolio can be viewed. Other sites ask for the username and password, but give you an option of clicking a box that instructs the Web site to "remember" this information so that you don't have to type it in every time you visit. What happens in this case is that the Web site reads a cookie on your computer with your username and password and immediately gives you access to your portfolio whenever you visit. If other people use your computer and you you're uncomfortable with the idea of them viewing your portfolio, then do not click on the "remember my password" button.

Online Investing

When you buy stocks through an online broker, you are transmitting highly personal financial information over the Internet. There is a theoretical risk of someone reading this information while in transit, but I consider it to be minimal enough that you don't have to worry about it. The reason is that the vast majority of online brokers require that clients have Web browsers equipped with what's called 128-bit encryption. This is heavy-duty security software that creates roadblocks that are virtually impassable to hackers.

If the version of Netscape Navigator or Microsoft Internet Explorer that you have on your computer has the less rigorous (but still effective) 40-bit encryption, you can easily download a version with 128-bit encryption over the Internet for free on the Netscape or Microsoft Web sites. As a bonus, you'll usually be able to download the most recent version of your browser at the same time as you boost your browser's security.

Where to Get 128-Bit Encryption

For Netscape Navigator users:

Go to www.netscape.com and click on "Browser Central."

For Internet Explorer users:

Go to www.microsoft.com/windows/ie/default.htm ∎

How to Be an Effective Online Investor

I have two pieces of advice for you here, and they may seem contradictory at first. Be open-minded to all the Internet has to offer you as an investor and, at the same time, be sceptical of everything you read. As you read through this book, you're going to be continually amazed at the depth and quality of investing information available on the Web. I know I was as I researched the book, and I continue to be today. Use the information you find online. Exploit it. Put it to work in every investing decision you make, so that you're always working from a position of knowledge.

At the same time, understand that there's little on the Internet that you can take at face value. Did you read something on a Web site in which an analyst calls a particular stock a "strong buy" and praises it to the sky? Be cautious because analysts aren't always unbiased in their views. It's not uncommon for investment dealers to provide advisery and underwriting services to the very same companies their analysts cover. Maybe an analyst can maintain objectivity in this situation, maybe not.

Did you find an interesting news story about a company on a Web site? Be sceptical because some of what looks like news at first glance is really a corporate news release in which news is spun to make a company look as good as possible. If a company announces something important, by all means read its news release. Then look for a story by a financial news service or newspaper to cut through the PR haze and tell you what really happened.

Understanding where information on financial Web sites comes from is crucially important in assessing its value, so let's take a close look at the sources you're likely to encounter.

Quotes: The usual arrangement is for a Web site to buy its quotes from a data services company that in turn obtains the information from the major stock exchanges.

Charts: Some Web sites have their own in-house charting software, while others use the technology developed by leaders in the field such as BigCharts.

News: Basic investing Web sites will almost always offer a selection of the day's top financial news stories, including stock market updates and corporate news. You'll find that most of this material comes from news services like Dow Jones, Reuters, Bloomberg, The Canadian Press, and Associated Press, all of which can be considered reliable from the point of view of a small investor who simply wants to get the lowdown on this or that news development. Keep in mind that you're not getting analysis here, just the facts and possibly some background and context.

You may also find sites out there that incorporate news from newspapers like *The Wall Street Journal* or *The Globe and Mail*. Check to see whether the news you're reading was taken from the actual newspaper or from the online news services maintained by these and other major news organizations. Stories from the newspaper would have been written the previous day so that they could appear in the morning newspaper. Web material is likely fresher, possibly written just minutes ago, but it's also bound to be shorter and thus shallower.

Some Web sites, CBS MarketWatch would be a perfect example, do their own news coverage. You'll have to judge the value of these news reports by reading them and assessing the knowledge level of the in-house reporters (I'd have no worries about MarketWatch, by the way). A few financial Web sites have earned such a solid reputation for their market coverage that other sites use their material. For example, several sites use the U.S. stock market commentary of Briefing.com, which is one of the 50 essential sites in this book.

News Releases: There are several different corporate news release services and they all do basically the same job in taking official company news and distributing it to the public. This is news from the company's point of view, unfiltered by reporters. In Canada, one of the biggest names in corporate news is Canada NewsWire, while others are Canadian Corporate News and BCE Emergis E-News Services. In the United States, a firm called PR Newswire is a dominant distributor of corporate news.

Analyst Consensus Ratings and Estimates: Dozens of investing Web sites offer this information, but there are only a handful of sources. One is Zacks, proprietor of Zacks.com, an excellent investing Web site listed in this book. Another major supplier is Thomson Financial Solutions, a huge financial data company that includes the Web site ThomsonFN.com among its services. ThomsonFN.com is also among the essential 50 Web sites.

UNBIASED STOCK RESEARCH

Many investing Web sites will tell you what brokerage analysts think about various stocks, and this can be quite a useful service. But I suggest you look at some unbiased research as well when sizing up a stock. What you have to understand is that the brokerage industry is not simply in the business of providing research. Brokerages often have business relationships as advisers or underwriters with the companies their analysts cover. Add the fact that the brokerage business thrives on stock trading and you end up with a decidedly bullish bias on most stock research. If there were a theme song for analysts, it would be Accentuate the Positive.

Brokerage firms are increasingly being called upon to disclose potential conflicts of interest in their stock research, and to give analysts more latitude to be objective. Still, unbiased research is an essential counterpoint to the work of analysts. To be able to write unbiased research, an analyst has to work for a firm that has no business relationship with the companies being researched. Some people think it's preferable that the analyst not own the stock being researched, and many Web sites recognize this by prohibiting their analysts from holdings stocks they cover. On other sites, analysts or columnists may hold stocks they write about, but they have to disclose this clearly in every column.

Here are eight sites included in this book where you can find unbiased equity research:

- Morningstar.com (www.morningstar.com)
- IDEAadviser (www.streetadviser.com)
- Wright Investors' Service (www.wisi.com)
- Worldlyinvestor.com (www.worldlyinvestor.com)
- TheStreet.com (www.thestreet.com)
- The Motley Fool (www.fool.com)
- Advice for Investors (www.adviceforinvestors.com)
- Briefing.com (www.briefing.com)

Here are another four Web sites that will help you find independent research. A brief description of each has been included:

Vickers Stock Research Corp. (www.argusgroup.com/reports.html) This site lists thousands of reports on U.S. and some inter-listed Canadian companies that can be sent either by fax or read online using an Adobe Acrobat reader. The reports are priced in units, which cost $3 (U.S.) apiece if you buy them individually and less if you buy them in bulk. Reports generally cost one to three units (free sample reports are available for General Electric). The Vickers catalogue includes Argus stock reports, which contain "buy"/"sell"/

"hold" recommendations and are updated on a daily basis, as events warrant. Argus, which has been around since 1934, stresses that it does no underwriting or trading, so its material is unbiased. Argus can also provide Standard & Poor's Stock Reports and Ford Value Graphs.

Value Line (www.valueline.com)
This respected stock analysis firm has been around for more than 50 years. About 1,700 companies are covered in a database that is updated on an ongoing basis. Each stock receives a thorough over-all analysis, as well as ratings on safety and timeliness. On a weekly basis, the Value Line investment survey takes each of the 1,700 stocks and ranks them on how they're likely to do over the next six to 12 months. Value Line subscriptions are pricey - $570 (U.S.) for a year of reports available online, on CD-ROM, or in print, $55 for a 10-week trial.

The Canadian Shareowners Association (www.shareowner.ca)
This group's purpose is to help small investors learn to tell the difference between, as the association itself puts it, great stocks and grief stocks. Members (the cost is $89 Canadian a year) receive the bimonthly magazine *Canadian Shareowner*, which includes analyses of a couple of stocks. Expect a detailed discussion of the company's prospects for revenue and earnings growth, and charts that suggest prices to buy, sell, and hold the stock. The CSA also sells its research and educational software on CD-ROM— the cost ranges from $49.95 to $199, depending on which product you buy. There's also an online database that you can use on a pay-as-you-go basis.

Kaiser Bottom-Fishing Report (www.canspecresearch.com)
Hungering for opinions on tiny companies like Takla Star Resources Ltd., Knexa.com Enterprises Inc., and DSI Datotech Systems Inc.? Then check out John Kaiser's newsletter on high-risk speculative stocks traded on the Canadian Venture Exchange, or CDNX. Each issue is written in a stream-of-consciousness style that is oddly appealing. Kaiser knows his stuff and it's obvious. He may own the shares he's writing about. Use the Web site mentioned above to

view previous issues of the Bottom-Fishing Report. Subscriptions are $199 (U.S.) or $499 for the deluxe version.

THE LAWLESS WEB

There are two things that make the Internet a nirvana for scammers—anonymity and reach. Any idiot can set up a Web site to sell a worthless product, bait the hook with a nice design and convincing words and then launch into cyberspace. The list of potential victims is as long as the number of people with Internet access. You have to be on guard for this whenever you're surfing the Web, but much more so where financial Web sites are concerned. What's the underlying theme on financial Web sites? Money—how to manage what you have and, more important, how to make more. This is the most fertile ground imaginable for rip-offs and fraud.

Here are some ways in which you have to be particularly cautious:

Online Message Boards

Some of the shrewdest investors you'll ever come across use these message boards, but so do some of the most dishonest ones. That's why you have to be very vigilant about whom and what you listen to. If someone's hyping an obscure stock, be more than careful. It's not unknown of for someone to try and generate a buzz about a junk stock in order to pump it up, then dump a big chunk of the shares. The stock price inevitably plunges in such situations, leaving the hapless people who bought on hype with holdings that are essentially worthless.

Even the shares of large companies can be moved by factually incorrect gossip or flagrantly fraudulent news releases disseminated by sociopathic investors with a grudge. The point is, be careful. When you read something very positive or negative about a stock, ask yourself whether the person posting the message has anything to gain if you act on these observations.

How to Spot a Scammer

The StockHouse Canada Web site (www.stockhouse.ca) offers these nine red flags to help spot message board scammers:

1. Someone who hyper-posts on only one stock.
During the promotional run of that stock, the user may be posting between 8 and 20 messages daily (sometimes more). The user will promote a stock for only so long, usually until he has sold his position or until he has fulfilled his obligation to the company that may have contracted his services.

2. Someone who uses multiple identities.
This is hard to detect. Generally, the poster will run with one identity until he has become despised on the message boards. Then, he will register again with a new identity. If one carefully studies such an individual, it will be found that he/she posts repeatedly about the same set of stocks, or just one stock. The poster will post during the same time each day or night. His messages will usually be the same length. His writing style will be similar and he will use the same phrases or key words in his messages.

3. Someone who repeatedly attacks or belittles others on a stock's message boards.
This goes beyond the simple heated debate with one or two members who disagree. If you carefully read his messages, this user will sound like he is fighting for his life with nearly everyone who challenges him.

4. Someone who emerges as the stock's moderator, or even the leader of the discussion group on that stock
This person is different from someone who has a genuine fundamental understanding of the company. A promoter/leader will diligently answer virtually every negative comment made on "his" message board. He will also cheerlead every positive comment and constantly make an appearance on the message board to "show" he is still the boss.

5. Someone, with a short history in their member profile, who suddenly shows up during a stock run-up, and appears to know "all about" the company.
This person is different from the excited investor, who just bought shares in the company and is enthusiastic about it. This kind of poster hints at "inside information" and quickly name-drops some connection to a company

cont'd

insider or employee. While the "excited" investor may rave about something an investor relations employee told him, the impostor hints at important, but as of yet unannounced, development(s) that may impact the stock price.

6. Someone who is nearly always the first to respond to company developments.

Occasionally, someone else will beat him to it. Otherwise, he's first or a close second almost every time. Commonly, he will positively spin the news, to soften the blow of bad news or to make good news appear better than it actually is.

7. Someone who continuously hints at upcoming company developments, unreleased company news and unannounced contracts.

Where did he get his information? Usually, he is the one who starts the rumour and might often state that he heard it from someone else.

8. Someone who hypes the company during the run-up and then "changes" his mind and begins attacking the company, its insiders and the project.

This individual carefully controls his statements, both up the chart and back down. On the way up, he may help the stock move higher by adding to the cheerleading, so that he can build a substantial short position. Once he changes his mind, he sticks with it.

9. Someone who goes out of their way to find bad news about the company and makes a "case" out of it.

These individuals might include ex-friends, ex-family (divorced) and ex-employees. Such people don't just post a single negative item. These individuals either take one negative news angle and make it look like "the sky is falling" or they continuously raise it. Frequent appearances by individuals who vent their spleen are a clue that gives them away. Disgruntled investors usually move on and don't want to be reminded of their bad investment.

These red flags are by no means a complete list of warning signs and should only be used as a guideline to help pinpoint fraudulent messages and posters.

In closing, it is important to note that not all fraudulent posters are bullish—some post messages to drive stock prices lower because of a vendetta or to profit by short selling. ■

The power of online rumours and gossip on Web discussion forums to influence stock prices is considerable. The public relations firm Fleishman-Hillard conducted a survey in 2001 of 120 public companies in Canada and around the world, asking them their views about the impact of the Internet. Sixty per cent of participants said that Internet chat and rumours can have an impact on their share price, while one-third said an investment professional or analyst had asked them about information or rumours related to their company on the Internet.

Newsletters and Stock-Picking Services

I've been sucked in by these products a few times. Usually, it was a case where I was looking around an entirely legitimate Web site and clicked on an ad saying something like "Ten Top Stock Picks for the Year Ahead." Next thing I knew, I'd find myself reading a pitch to subscribe to a stock-picking newsletter that inevitably boasted quadruple-digit returns and zero risk. Cost: $750 (U.S.) per year, or something like that.

I've never subscribed to any of these newsletters or stock-picking services and I've never been tempted to. I recognize that some of these services may offer solid, professional recommendations, but I also find the exaggerated claims and hokey salesmanship of many newsletters to be laughable. I'd no more trust most of these publications than I would a stock tip written on a bathroom stall. Maybe you'll find a trustworthy newsletter someday that turns your crank—that's great, but be sure to check into the credibility and reliability of the publication first.

Plain Old Scams

The same ingenuity and ruthlessness that scammers have brought to the telemarketing field are in evidence on the Internet. We're talking here about fraudulent, non-existent products and services that are dangled out there in cyberspace for no other reason than to catch an unsuspecting sucker. I find it hard to believe these suckers exist, but they do. The very fact that such scams are being run is a testament to the existence of these naïve, trusting souls, but there's more concrete evidence as well.

Not too long ago, the Ontario Securities Commission set up a phony Web site to demonstrate the risks of blindly buying into information found on the Internet. The professional-looking site was called www.noriskwealth.ca and it offered monthly returns of as much as 30 per cent by investing in "international debentures" that were eligible for registered retirement savings plans. To stir up interest in the site, newspaper advertisements were placed, and postings made to Internet chat rooms. It all sounds farcical, except for one thing. Over a span of six weeks, there were 126 requests for information on www.noriskwealth.ca. According to the OSC, several people were willing to immediately fork over their money.

In announcing the results of this pseudo-sting, Michael Watson, the OSC's director of enforcement, offered advice that we've all heard before a million times. Many people obviously need to hear it again, so here it is: "...If it looks too good to be true, it probably is," Mr. Watson said. "Anything that says it's a no-risk high-return investment is likely a fraud."

CANADA VERSUS THE UNITED STATES

Sooner or later, it's going to hit you. While there's an ocean's worth of information about U.S. stocks on the Web, there's a mere puddle for Canadian stocks. Heard of the Rule of 10? It stipulates that you can arrive at a Canadian equivalent of any U.S. statistic by dividing by 10. For investing Web sites, divide by 20, or maybe even 50. One of the most common questions I hear from people about investing Web sites is, Where can I find this or that type of information for *Canadian* stocks? Often, I have to say the information's just not available.

The really frustrating thing here is that there has been a marked deterioration in the quantity and quality of financial Web sites aimed at Canadians. From the late 1990s through to early 2000, there was a real flowering of these sites. In addition to market leader Globeinvestor.com, we had StockHouse Canada, Canada iNvest, Stockformation, and quite a few others. Then came the dotcom crash. Beset by a plunge in online advertising and an inability to raise new funds, many sites packed it in. Globeinvestor.com remains, while StockHouse Canada still existed as this book went to press, but in a somewhat diminished form. StockHouse is included among the 50 essential sites because of a couple of excellent features it offers, but its usefulness rating has plunged from five to two.

StockHouse's decline makes for a nice little case study in how investors have become informationally impoverished by what has happened to the Canadian financial Web sector. First, StockHouse offered a running list throughout the day of Canadian stocks that had had their ratings upgraded, downgraded, or reiterated by analysts. As I wrote this book, I was unable to find a single other Canadian site that offered the same highly useful information. As well, StockHouse often interviewed mutual fund managers to quiz them on their stock picks. You can find this kind of content on other sites, notably InvestorCanada, but it's still missed on StockHouse. The biggest loss on StockHouse was the regular columns on subjects like Canadian technology and oil and gas stocks, and Canadian stocks that looked interesting from a technical point of view. Canadian Web sites were always weakest on original commentary and analysis, and now they're all the more so.

If there's any good news here, it's that many U.S. sites offer quotes, charts, analyst opinions, and earnings estimates on Canadian companies that are cross-listed on U.S. and Canadian exchanges. A small number, among them MSN Money and BigCharts, also include data on stocks listed only on Canadian exchanges. My conclusion is that U.S. Web companies are starting to realize that there are enough Canadian online investors out there to make the effort worthwhile. As well, a growing number of American investors are starting to wake up to the fact that there are some attractive stocks to be found in Canada.

Another area where U.S. Web sites differ from Canadian ones is in the ancillary financial services they offer. Take a look at Yahoo Finance and you'll see what I mean. Yahoo offers online bill payments and fund transfers, as well as a service that connects all your various online bank, credit card, and brokerage accounts to a single log-in. Another example is MSN Money, which offers a service that provides personalized retirement portfolio recommendations tailored to your personal profile. Yahoo, MSN Money, and some other U.S. financial sites have also partnered up with online brokers, creating "trade now" links that take you from information about a stock to a page where you can learn more or sign-up for an online brokerage account. (Some of these promotions have raised concerns that the lines are being blurred between financial Web sites and actual brokers and banks. The issue has even caught the attention of the U.S. Securities and Exchange Commission.)

FREE SERVICES VERSUS PAY SERVICES

Almost all the sites mentioned in this book offer significant resources at no charge, and a decided majority are 100 per cent free. Several sites have a subscription-based premium service that builds on the no-cost basic product in one way or another—if you like the basic service, you may well feel the deluxe product is worth the expenditure. Other sites—Multex Investor would be a good example—sell research on a piece-by-piece basis.

To Pay or Not to Pay

Never sign up for a service or product on an investing Web site that charges a fee without first trying out the merchandise. Many reputable services will let you sign up for a free trial, and I strongly suggest you take advantage. As you're testing the service, ask yourself how useful the information is to you and whether you're likely to profit from it in a way that would justify the expense.

Often, these pay services are based on proprietary research or strategies that come with extravagant claims about outperforming the major stock market indexes. Don't just take these claims for granted. Look for documentation, and then examine the research itself to see if it's credible. Also, check to see whether reputable investing magazines have ever written about the service. If a site's been mentioned in *Fortune* or *Business Week*, it's a guarantee they'll tell you. ■

In the future, look for more and more financial Web sites to charge for their content, or to offer basic services for free and hold back their best stuff for paying subscribers. It's sad to say, but the business model in which Web sites charge for online advertising but give content away is a failure. As this book was being written, financial Web sites were only just beginning to figure out how to operate in this new reality. Globeinvestor.com was due at presstime to introduce a premium version of the site for paying subscribers, while SmartMoney.com had already done likewise. At Yahoo Finance, one of the best totally free investing Web sites out there, they've introduced the Yahoo Real-Time Package, which offered streaming stock quotes and other premium services for a monthly charge of $9.95 (U.S.). Yahoo has also come out with a service that allows you to buy stock research from major brokerage houses. Note that Yahoo hadn't withdrawn any of its free content, just augmented it with better material for people willing to pay the price. This seems to be a fair way of doing things.

A Quick Guide to the 50 Essential Financial Web Sites

If the idea of auditioning 50 Web sites to find the ones right for you sounds a little overwhelming, then let's simplify things. In this chapter, we'll look at the various categories of financial Web site and the actual sites in this book that belong to each one. As well, you'll find a list of the best site or sites for a wide variety of investor needs—say, the best site for explaining complex investing jargon or the best site for independent stock research.

TYPES OF FINANCIAL WEB SITES

Directories: These sites are mainly a collection of links to other investing Web sites. The directory sites in this book are:

- EquityWeb
- Investing:Canada
- 100hot
- Site-By-Site.

Educational: Sites that teach you about investing and personal finance or explain related terms and concepts. The applicable sites in this book are:

- Investopedia.com
- Investor Learning Centre.

Message Boards: Sites that specialize in online discussions between investors. These sites are distinct from the many financial Web sites that offer message boards as a sideline. The message board sites included here are:

- Silicon Investor
- TheLion.com

Mutual Funds: These sites focus on mutual funds primarily, although they may also look at stocks and personal finance. The fund sites here are:

- FundLibrary.com
- Globefund.com
- Morningstar.ca

Portals, or Megasites: These are all-in-one sites that combine news, stock quotes and research tools, personal finance information, online portfolio tracking, and so on. The portals in this book are:

- Briefing.com
- CBS MarketWatch
- CNET
- MSN Money
- The Motley Fool
- Quicken.ca
- Quicken.com
- SmartMoney.com
- TheStreet.com
- Yahoo Finance.

Research/Stock Picking: These sites can be used to help you research stocks, or to provide you with investing ideas:

- ADR.com
- Advice For Investors
- Canadian Business
- ClearStation
- Globeinvestor.com
- IDEAadvisor
- Individual Investor
- InvestorCanada
- Morningstar.com
- Multex Investor
- Nasdaq
- Stingy Investor
- StockHouse
- ThomsonFN.com
- Validea
- Value Investigator
- Worldlyinvestor.com
- Wright Investors' Service
- Zacks.com

Specialty Sites: These sites perform a unique function such as charting or technical analysis or risk assessment. The specialty sites included here are:

- BigCharts
- IndexFunds
- InvestinginBonds.com
- ON24
- Q1234.com

- RiskGrades
- SEDAR
- SEDI
- StockCharts.com
- Stockscores.

Now, let's look at the best sites for all kinds of different needs.

The best sites for novice investors: The Motley Fool, MSN Money

The best site for explaining complex investing terms: Investopedia.com

The best sites for historical data on stocks: BigCharts (historical quotes), MSN Money, and Advice For Investors (historical ratios)

The best day-to-day intelligence on what's going on in the major U.S. markets: Briefing.com, CBS MarketWatch, TheStreet.com

The best all-around investing site for Canadians: Globeinvestor.com

The best general-purpose personal finance site for Canadians: Quicken.ca

The best mutual fund site: Morningstar.ca

The best source of information on exchange-traded funds: IndexFunds

The best site for aficionados of technical analysis: ClearStation, StockCharts.com

The site with the easiest-to-use stock screening tool: MSN Money

The site with the coolest online tools: SmartMoney.com

The handiest all-around investing site: Yahoo Finance

The best sites for independent, unbiased stock research: Morningstar.com (U.S. stocks), Advice For Investors (Canadian stocks)

The best site to keep up with stock prices in after-hours trading: Yahoo Finance

Two surprisingly useful sites: Nasdaq.com, RiskGrades

ADR.com

What's the Deal?:
Your go-to Web site for researching hundreds of international companies that you can invest in as American Depositary Receipts traded on
the New York Stock Exchange.

Usefulness Rating: ✓✓✓✓

Canadian Content Rating: not applicable

Cost: Free

Every so often, you're bound to come across a foreign company
that sounds like a great investing opportunity. For me, the Finnish
company Nokia was an example at one time. In the wireless phone
market, Nokia ruled. Sure, the company had some mighty competitors, notably Motorola and Ericsson. But while these firms
always seemed to be fighting adversity in one form or another,
Nokia cruised along in comparatively solid shape. Nobody was calling cell phones "Nokias" yet, but it seemed a distinct possibility.

Now, how would one go about participating in Nokia's success,
I wondered. Probably about a zillion global mutual funds held
Nokia, but I was curious about the idea of owning the shares

directly. That was a problem because no brokerage I knew offered trading on the Helsinki Stock Exchange. Fortunately, Nokia's shares are listed on the New York Stock Exchange as American Depositary Receipts, or ADRs. Think of ADRs as you would any other U.S. stock. They can be bought and sold through any broker, full-service or discount, and many can easily be researched on the Internet. More specifically, they can be easily be researched on the Web site ADR.com.

ADR.com is run by J.P. Morgan, the big U.S. investment dealer, and it is the ideal place to start looking if you want to globally diversify your stock portfolio. For an overview of ADRs, try clicking on the "ADR Market" button at the top of the homepage. There, you'll find a list of the day's Top 10 ADRs by trading volume. Among the stocks to appear often on the list are Nokia, Ericsson of Sweden, Britain's Vodafone Airtouch, the Netherlands' Royal Dutch Petroleum, Alcatel of France, and Taiwan Semiconductor. Want to know which ADRs are most widely held by U.S. institutional investors or, in other words, the investing pros who are supposed to know what stocks are worth holding? The information is right there. I found— what else?—Nokia at the top of the list. You can also use ADR.com to find the Top 10 ADRs that institutional investors were both buying and selling over the previous quarter. I found Nokia at the top of the buy list and Britain's BP Amoco at the top of the sell list.

ADR.com also allows you to search for ADRs by company name, by region and by industry. You could, for example, find Israeli companies with NYSE-listed ADRs (I found seven), or you could comb the world for ADRs in the beverage or steel industries. For steel producers, I found 12 companies listed from Brazil, Mexico, Korea, Chile, Taiwan, the Netherlands, and Britain.

Each day, the ADR.com homepage offers a list of the day's top-performing ADR stocks and industrial sectors, and a list of news stories about ADR companies. There's also daily coverage of the broad ADR market, which seems a bit odd given that it lumps together all kinds of companies that have nothing in common other than the fact that their stocks trade as ADRs.

What Are ADRs and How Do They Work?

ADRs are a great tool for the investor who wants international diversification without having to go to the trouble and expense of dealing with foreign stock exchanges and foreign currencies. An international mutual fund will serve you better than just holding a couple of different ADRs. But if you want to augment your foreign fund with individual stock picks, or replace the fund with a broad selection of global stocks, then ADRs are the way to go.

When you own a company's ADR, what you've really got is a certificate issued by a bank holding the actual shares of that company. Two of the biggest ADR banks are the Bank of New York and J.P. Morgan, which issued the first ADRs back in 1927 to give U.S. investors a chance to own the shares of a British retailer called Selfridge's. One thing to keep in mind when buying ADRs is that each depositary receipt can represent several shares of the underlying company, or a fraction of a share. A Vodafone ADR represents 10 shares of the company, a Nokia ADR represents a single share, and an ADR of the French insurance company AXA equals half a share.

ADRs are traded in U.S. dollars and track the price moves of their underlying stock, but there can be deviations that result from currency exchange rates and other factors. These imbalances are kept in line by arbitragers, who profit by buying a security or its equivalent on one stock exchange and then instantly selling it on another. High-profile ADRs such as Nokia and Royal Dutch Petroleum usually trade on the NYSE, Nasdaq, or the American Stock Exchange. Some ADRs aren't listed on a major exchange and instead trade on the over-the-counter (OTC) market.

ADRs are increasingly popular these days because of the demand for more international investing opportunities, and because foreign companies want the exposure to North American markets. ■

The ADR world includes some of the most prominent global corporations, so there's lots of research material out there for investors on most any major investing Web site. ADR.com offers a good package of research tools as well. Just type a stock symbol into the ticker box on the homepage and you can get a quick overview of an ADR stock, a list of recent news stories that mention the stock, recent financial statements and financial ratios, charts, earnings estimates, and consensus recommendations from analysts, and links to the company's own Web pages.

Many investors think only of Canada and the United States when picking stocks for their portfolios. With ADRs, you can be a little more worldly.

ADR.COM AT A GLANCE:

Who's It For?
Investors who are interested in buying the shares of foreign companies.

Top Things to Do on This Site:
1. Find out which global companies are available to North American investors as ADRs.
2. Research foreign companies of interest.
3. Find out which ADRs are available by sector, or country.

Don't Miss:
The lists of the most popular ADRs.

Toys:
1. Create an online ADR portfolio that will give you quotes and news. You can also rig the portfolio to e-mail you end-of-day prices for the stocks in your portfolio, as well as alerts about price moves in your stocks.
2. You can set up an ADR stock ticker that runs across the bottom of the ADR.com homepage.

LINKS

Site-By-Site (www.site-by-site.com): This Web site gathers together an amazing array of investing links from virtually every country in the world with a stock exchange. If you want to research global stocks and stock markets, Site-By-Site may be the only Web site you need.

Worldlyinvestor.com (www.worldlyinvestor.com): This independent stock research site mainly covers U.S. stocks, but it also offers weekly columns on emerging market stocks, Asian stocks, and European stocks.

Financial Times (www.ft.com): The venerable *Financial Times* newspaper's Web site provides global coverage of economics and market developments. There is also extensive emerging market coverage, plus detailed coverage of the U.S., British, Asian, and European stock markets.

Advice For Investors

www.adviceforinvestors.com

What's the Deal?:
A pay Web site for investors who want access to a vast library of unbiased stock research and research tools.

Usefulness Rating: ✓✓✓✓✓

Canadian Content Rating: ✓✓✓✓✓

Cost: Minimal free services; cost of pay services varies—see details below.

M y personal policy on pay Web sites comes down to three words: Forget about it. There's enough useful free stuff out there that I just don't feel the need to pay for research or services. Every so often, though, I come across a site that tests my resolve. One of them is Advice For Investors.

There are two ways this site excels—in the sophistication of its investing tools, and in the depth of the stock research it provides. Advice For Investors is produced by MPL Communications, which describes itself as Canada's largest provider of independent investment research. Maybe you've heard of some of their publications. One is *The Investment Reporter*, which began in 1941 and is still going strong. Another is *Investor's Digest of Canada*, a tabloid investing newspaper that is sold at most magazine stores, while still another is the *Blue Book of Stock Reports*. All are full of clear, well-argued, conservative advice tailored for the buy-and-hold portfolios of Jane and Joe Investor. If you subscribe to Advice For Investors, you get to tap into this vast pool of MPL stock research, plus the work of outside analysts. The net result is that you're likely to find a variety of views on the vast majority of stocks listed on the Toronto Stock Exchange.

Advice For Investors' Pay Services

Before you buy, try. This is always a good policy with pay services offered on financial Web sites, providing they offer free or cut-rate trials. Advice For Investors has in the past offered a five-week trial for $4.37. The regular subscription rate is $97 per year, plus $10 apiece for any Blue Book stock reports you download. You can buy a one-year subscription to the Blue Book reports that allows unlimited access for $97. ■

Let's say you were curious about Bracknell Corp., a company that designs and builds systems and networks for big corporate clients. The first thing you would do after logging in as an Advice For Investors is subscriber would be to click the "Research" button on the homepage and then type in Bracknell's stock symbol, BRK. When I tried this, I found a Blue Book report on Bracknell with a $10 price tag. I downloaded the one-page report in a few seconds (I used high-speed Internet access; with regular service it could take a few minutes). It turned out that Bracknell was rated a "buy" by MPL analysts. Key ratios were provided in the report, as were financial data and a company outlook. Note: At press time, Advice For Investors was to add up-to-the-minute financial data to Blue Book reports. Previously, the numbers were updated only periodically.

For more information on Bracknell, head to the "Stocks" area of the site and call up a company profile. Next, click on the "Advice Articles" tab and take a look at the recent mentions of Bracknell on the Advice For Investors site. I found three mentions, one in an article about a month old and two that were several months old. Two of the articles were written by MPL staff, while one was extracted from research by an analyst with TD Securities.

Let's say that you like what you've seen of Bracknell, but you want to check what other stocks are mentioned on Advice For Investors. The best thing to do in this case is click where it says "Advice" on the homepage. The Advice area is divided into six sections: Advice from MPL's own analysts, research from outside analysts, mutual fund advice, advice from MPL newsletters, advice on bonds and fixed income investments, and money management advice. Under each heading is a brief overview and a link to the full article. Here's a partial inventory of articles I found one day:

- *The Investment Reporter's* "Best Buy" stocks for the month.
- A recommendation to accumulate the shares of two junior biotechnology companies.
- Guidance on picking stocks in the auto sector.
- The outlook for Cogeco Cable.
- A recommendation to consider investing in the Templeton Growth Fund.
- An extract from an *Investor's Digest* article highlighting three Canadian high tech stocks that had been mentioned in a U.S. investing newsletter.
- A recommendation to consider buying provincial bonds over guaranteed investment certificates and treasury bills.
- A look at how deposit insurance works on accounts held at credit unions.

You can't accuse MPL of not giving paying customers their money's worth because you will find several new stories put on the Web site each day. Moreover, stories are left up for months, so you can also visit periodically and catch up on what you missed.

Searching for Stocks

After reading through the "Advice" section of the Web site, you might decide to widen your search for interesting stocks by using the stock-screening and comparison tools.

Stock Screening: I think this screener is one of the better ones available on the Web. There are others that are far more sophisticated in the screening criteria they give you, but the Advice For Investors version makes up for this with an intelligent design. You'll find the screener divided into two sections, one for fundamental criteria and another for technical criteria. The fundamentals you can screen for include annual revenue, assets, price-earnings ratio, earnings per share, and share price. For each, you can specify a range, as in a P/E ratio higher than five but lower than 20.

The technical section of the screener is especially well designed because you don't have to be an expert on the arcane world of technical analysis to use it. For instance, you can set the screener to find stocks with an MACD that shows a buy or sell signal. I know enough about technical analysis to be aware that MACD stands for moving average convergence/divergence, but I haven't a clue how to really use this indicator. With the Advice For Investors screener, all the work is done for me.

Stock Comparisons: Ever wanted to compare ratios or financials for a group of stocks? On most Web sites, you have to research one stock, then another, then another. What a pain. With Advice For Investors, you can choose up to five stocks and create side-by-side comparisons in such areas as key ratios, balance sheets, income statements, cashflow, and historical financials. Trying to decide which of the Big Five banks to buy? This feature would definitely help. ∎

Now, let's get back to Bracknell. To continue your investigation of the stock, head back to the "Stocks" area of the site. Type BRK into the "Company Profile" tickerbox and then follow this step-by-step game plan:

1. First up, click on the "Short Positions" tab. Investors shorting a stock are betting that it will decline in price. If there is significant short interest in Bracknell, or if there has been a recent

increase in short interest, this could be a negative indicator about the stock's near-term prospects. Bracknell registered a decline in short interest.

2. Next, click on "Insider Trading." If company insiders are buying, that's a bullish signal; if they're selling, that may be a warning sign. Advice For Investors showed no recent insider trades, but it did list a series of buy transactions over the previous year.

3. The "Analyst Ratings" section is next. This is a widely available service elsewhere on the web, but Advice For Investors gives you a little more detail than you'll get from most other sources. For example, it will give you analysts' 12-month price targets and tell you in a few cases how individual brokerages rate a stock. The outlook for Bracknell was hard to read because analysts seemed to be losing interest in the stock. Whereas three analysts had rated it a few months earlier, the latest consensus had only one analyst participating.

4. Now, click on "Historical Financials" to view key financial ratios for Bracknell, as well as income statements, balance sheets, and so on. You can view the numbers in a table format or graph them. The graphing function here is tremendous in that you can compare up to five different stocks in one particular area— say their price-earnings ratio—or you can graph up to five different types of information for one stock at a time.

Given that it's primarily a pay Web site, the onus is on Advice For Investors to provide better investing tools than free sites. You've probably already gathered that Advice For Investors delivers on this count, but if you are looking for more evidence, consider the site's portfolio tracker. It's easy to use, sharply designed and, most important, packed with useful information about your stocks. You set up a portfolio—you can have as many as five different ones—by selecting a name for your group of stocks and deciding what currency you want. Then, just type the symbols of the stocks you've bought, as well as the purchase price, quantity, and purchase date.

Once your portfolio is up and running, you can get updates throughout the trading day by clicking where it says "Portfolio" on the homepage, and then selecting the portfolio you want to view. The first thing you'll see is a pie graph with a slice for each stock in your portfolio. The graph is colour-coded in a way that instantly tells you how your portfolio as a whole is doing. Varying shades of blue show your portfolio is up, grey means it's flat, and shades of red denote losses. This feature is more a novelty than anything else, but it is eye-catching.

The business end of the Advice For Investors portfolio tracker can be found underneath the pie graph. At first glance, it looks like a standard portfolio chart with its listing of each stock and its current value as well as overall gains and losses. Look closer and you'll find that you can set up four different views of your holdings: Current status, tax information, transaction history, and analysis. Choose the tax information option and you'll see your portfolio's capital gains/losses, dividends, and income broken out separately. There's also a nifty capital gains calculator that is designed to tell you how much of a gain or loss you'll take if you sell a particular holding in your portfolio.

The analysis section of the portfolio tracker is unique as well. First, there's a pie graph of your portfolio showing the portions of your holdings that lie in five quality ratings ranging from speculative to very conservative. Another pie graph shows how much of your portfolio lies in various industry sectors. Together, these two graphs will help to make sure your holdings are properly diversified according to risk and industry.

The free area of Advice For Investors is reasonably useful, but it wouldn't come close to making the 50 essential sites in this book. The best feature is the library of Canadian company profiles. Key in a stock symbol or company name and you'll jump to a page with a company snapshot and a broad menu of links that will take you to a stock quote or chart, to the company's own Web site, and to recent company news releases. Better, there are links to a variety of outside research sites. For example, there's a link to the company's recent regulatory filings on the SEDAR Web site (an essential site listed in this book), and to a research report on the company by Wright Investors' Service. In a nice touch, Advice For Investors also provides a link to the Silicon Investor's message board on the company (both Wright and Silicon Investor are also essential sites in this book).

Despite these features, the free area of Advice For Investors is unpleasant to use because you keep bumping into services that are only available to paying customers. Advice For Investors tells you this by proclaiming: "The page you requested is available only to subscribers." If you encounter this a few times, you'll quickly conclude that the free services on Advice For Investors are mainly a billboard for the subscription services.

ADVICE FOR INVESTORS AT A GLANCE

Who's It For?
Investors willing to pay for access to a vast database of stock research, as well as a top-notch selection of research tools.

Top Things to Do on This Site:
1. Look up research reports on companies you're following.
2. Look for stock-picking ideas by reading the recommendations of in-house analysts and brokerage analysts.
3. Do more in-depth research by looking up ratios, insider trading data, and so on.

Don't Miss:
The portfolio tracker. It beats most others available on the Web.

Toys:
A daily e-mail service that gives you daily updates on all the stocks in your portfolio, including analysts' reports, press releases, insider trading reports, and short positions.

LINKS

Globeinvestor.com (www.globeinvestor.com): Part of *The Globe and Mail* newspaper's corporate family, this free site offers solid stock research tools, a sophisticated portfolio tracker, and access to a searchable archive of investing articles that have appeared in the newspaper.

Yahoo Finance (ca.finance.yahoo.com): One of the best all-around investing sites out there. Combines stock research tools, simple but useful portfolio tracking, and access to investing articles that have appeared on other Web sites.

BigCharts

www.bigcharts.com

What's the Deal?:
Customized stock charting that is more flexible, easier to use, and nicer to look at than most of the competition.

Usefulness Rating: ✓✓✓✓

Canadian Content Rating: ✓✓✓✓

Cost: Free

I was feeling a bit peeved as I wrote about this excellent Web site for charting stocks and stock markets. I knew there was a full database on Canadian stocks, but I couldn't remember the trick for getting the site to recognize the symbols for them. Every time I typed in a Canadian symbol, I'd get a list of American stocks with similar symbols. Then, I wasted some more time scouring the site's help function for assistance. No go. Finally, I happened onto the closely guarded secret of how to look up Canadian stocks: For quotes and charts, type CA: in front of the symbol, as in CA:HHL.A.

BigCharts is one of a few U.S. investing Web sites out there that take the trouble to include Canadian data, then don't bother to explain clearly how users can gain access. I could speculate on why this happens, but what's the point? Better to explain the extremely useful function that BigCharts performs. Succinctly speaking, this is one of the best tools out there for creating charts of a stock you're following, or of a particular stock index.

Let's say that Hurricane Hydrocarbons, symbol HHL.A on the Toronto Stock Exchange, has caught your eye and you want to see how it has done over the past 12 months. Choose the "Quickchart" option on the homepage and you'll get a one-year price and volume graph, along with a brief stock quote and a list of recent news stories. That's routine stuff, sure, but it's merely a warm-up to the real value of BigCharts—its interactive charts. To get rolling, click the "Java Chart" button. BigCharts will then produce a one-year chart for Hurricane, with notations to show the dates of dividends, share splits, and earnings reports (whether earnings were up or down is also noted). Next, move your cursor to any point along the chart. The software will tell you the open, high, low, and closing prices for Hurricane shares on that day. As you slide the cursor along horizontally, the share price information will change to reflect the day in question. The Java Charts function includes separate graphics for volume and a few different technical indicators, including MACD, or moving average convergence/divergence. To customize the charts, use the menu of options on the left side of the page.

While the Java Charts are a slick bit of technology, they're not as easy to customize as the graphs you can punch up using the "Interactive Chart" button on the homepage. Say you wanted to plot Hurricane's 200-day moving average to get an idea of the stock's long-term price momentum. Just click on the "indicators" button and select SMA, for simple moving average, then type the number 200 into the adjacent box. BigCharts also lets you compare two stocks, so let's add another stock to the mix, say Nexen Inc. (formerly Canadian Occidental Petroleum). From there, you can further customize your chart according to timeframe (from one day to "all data"), size (small, medium, large) and background display (will that be black and white, blue, or a graph paper motif, to name but a few of the choices). I suggest you choose the blue background—it looks striking and is easy to read.

When you're finished designing your chart, you simply click on the "Draw Chart" button or clear the chart settings and start over. When I created the Hurricane/Nexen graph, I found that Hurricane was riding a nice upward price wave and had gained about 75 per cent over the previous 12 months, outpacing Nexen and its gain of about 40 per cent. BigCharts is capable of a lot more than this, particularly in the area of technical analysis, but you get the idea.

Charting is commonly available on investing Web sites, but the graphic quality and easy flexibility offered by BigCharts is far above the norm. The site offers more than charts, however. Call up a Quickchart on a stock and you'll find links to relevant brokerage research available through Multex Investor (another of the 50 essential sites), as well as analyst consensus earnings estimates and insider trading reports. Caution: Canadian stocks are less well covered in this part of the BigCharts site. Other things you can do with BigCharts include calling up "BigReport" lists of the day's most active stocks on all major U.S. and Canadian stock exchanges, the biggest movers by percentage and dollar amounts, and the most actively traded stocks.

Another BigCharts option is to scan stocks by industry grouping. BigCharts uses the 10 Dow Jones industry sectors for the U.S. market—click on one and you'll see a list of subsectors that can in turn be broken down into a list of constituent stocks. One of the coolest toys on BigCharts is the "Historical Quotes" function. Want to know what Hurricane Hydrocarbons closed at on Dec. 12, 1994? BigCharts says the answer is $1.60, with an intra-day high and low of $1.85 and $1.60, respectively. I tried a few other stocks and found the database went back to 1987.

BigCharts also provides daily market commentary courtesy of its parent, financial megasite CBS MarketWatch (yet another of the 50 sites in this book), as well as news reports from Reuters. Just click on the "News" button on the homepage for a menu of news items. For repeat visitors, BigCharts lets you save your chart settings so that they become a default for all charts you create (you can cancel the settings either permanently or temporarily). The site also lets you create a favourites list that lets you return quickly to the charts of stocks you're following.

BIGCHARTS AT A GLANCE:

Who's It For?
Investors who need a stock-graphing tool that is more sophisticated than what is available on general-purpose investing Web sites; also, investors interested in technical analysis.

Top Things to Do on This Site:
1. Run stocks you're following through the charting machinery—guaranteed you'll know the stock a lot better after you do.

2. Dabble with technical analysis.

3. Find historical quotes unavailable on other investing Web sites.

Don't Miss:
BigReports, a list of the biggest movers on either U.S. or Canadian exchanges, complete with links to stock charts.

Toys:
1. The stock charts offered by BigCharts are endlessly adjustable, but if you find a particular arrangement that works well you can save it and use it as your default chart.

2. Chart favourites, a feature that allows you to create charts of particular stocks that are automatically updated whenever you open the BigCharts Web site.

LINKS

StockCharts.com (www.stockcharts.com): Sophisticated charting tools for investors interested in technical analysis.

Briefing.com

www.briefing.com

What's the Deal?:
Continuously updated analysis of what is happening on U.S. markets

Usefulness Rating: ✓✓✓✓

Canadian Content Rating: ✓

Cost: Comprehensive basic services are free; subscription fees are charged for premium service.

It's two minutes after 1 p.m. on a Friday afternoon and shares of RadioShack Corp. are plunging with surprising abandon for such an old war-horse retailer. What's the story? Briefing.com will tell you like few other Web sites. "This consumer electronics retailer shared some news with the market this morning, and one need only glance at its stock price to know that the news was negative," wrote Briefing.com analyst Patrick J. O'Hare. "RadioShack warned its fiscal Q1 earnings would be approximately $0.31-$0.33 per share, down from the $0.34 per share profit in the year-ago period and the First Call consensus estimate of $0.38. Although RSH didn't provide any specific details in its press release for the impending shortfall, it can be inferred that sales and gross margins weren't as robust as expected. The latter assumption stems from RSH's contention that for the balance of the year it will have a 'very keen focus on gross margin enhancement and expense reduction.'"

I've included this excerpt from the report on Radio Shack to give you a sense of how informed and opinionated the daily stock commentary is on Briefing.com. After dissecting Radio Shack and its earnings warning, Mr. O'Hare went on to say this: "Investors have wanted little to do with RSH today as the stock is down 21 per cent on more than three times its average daily volume. Frankly, Briefing.com thinks the market has overreacted to the warning. Subsequently, we would use the pullback to accumulate the stock, emboldened by the idea that even if RSH had zero EPS growth in fiscal 2001, it would still trade at an attractive 16.5 times estimated earnings—a P/E multiple that is near a five-year low."

As you may have gathered, Briefing.com is a service designed for active investors who want expert guidance on what the stock and bond markets are doing throughout the day. The hundreds of updates the site produces each day are, in the words of Briefing.com itself, designed to help you trade. Briefing.com describes its stories as "live market analysis," which means that market events are covered as they happen. It's an approach that makes for some of the most thorough stock market coverage you'll find on the Web. The same day Radio Shack tanked, Briefing.com started its market coverage at 6:32 a.m. with a quick note about what the Japanese Nikkei index and Hong Kong's Hang Seng were up to. From there, it swung into coverage of what the morning's futures trading indicated about the course of the North American stock market. The running commentary was updated about every 20 to 30 minutes in order to include developments like the morning's economic data. Once North American markets opened for trading at 9:30 a.m., Briefing.com provided updates every 30 minutes or so until the close, when a wrap-up story was written.

Lots of financial Web sites carry stock market updates, but they're usually written by harried reporters at financial wire services who dash them out by rote. Briefing.com takes an analytical tone to everything while also weaving in essential information like which stocks are moving the markets. Make that the U.S. markets —there is little coverage on Briefing.com on global markets, and Canadian markets are pretty much ignored.

Briefing.com's Analysts

One of the things that sets Briefing.com apart from other financial Web sites is the expertise of its in-house analysts. Many of these people are former senior managers and analysts from Standard & Poor's MMS International, a major online analysis firm. Briefing.com has its own chief economist, fixed income strategist, director of research, and chief equity analyst.

It also has to be noted that these experts are independent and therefore are much freer than brokerage analysts to say what they really think about stocks and the markets. Briefing.com does not allow its editors to speculate in the financial markets or write about stocks that they own. As well, Briefing.com itself takes no market positions. ■

Briefing.com's market coverage is top-notch, but the real action on the site is in its coverage of the day's hot stocks. There are quick one- or two-line summaries on each stock contained in a feature called "Short Stories," and longer write-ups contained in a section of the Web site called "Story Stocks." A feature called "In Play" provides additional stock coverage by focusing on stocks that are moving and may present trading opportunities. As well, the site provides a daily list of all stocks that have been upgraded or downgraded by analysts. Other sites provide similar listings, but Briefing.com's seem to be more complete in that they include the broker, the old rating, the new rating, and the price target for the stock. One other feature of note is Briefing.com's coverage of the bond market.

All the services described so far on Briefing.com are free—to access them, use the Web address at the top of the page and then click where it says "Free Services." One of the things I like best about Briefing.com is that even though it's very much a pay Web site, it still offers an excellent free service. At no time while using the free site do you click on links just to find yourself on a page that is only accessible to subscribers. Still, there's no doubt that Briefing.com does provide a better, more timely service to subscribers.

There are two subscription service packages:

Stock Analysis: Costs $9.95 (U.S.) per month or $100 per year and provides all the free services, but on a faster basis. For example, you get a continuously updated "In Play," rather than hourly updates. Stock upgrades and downgrades are provided as they happen—on the free site, you get updates three times a day. As well, this package includes technology stock analysis, an IPO calendar, and a searchable archive.

Professional: Costs $25 (U.S.) per month or $250 per year and includes the Stock Analysis services, plus additional focus on the bond market. Includes live bond and foreign exchange coverage, bond briefs, and analysis of economic developments and policies of the U.S. Federal Reserve.

Unless you've got a strong interest in the U.S. bond market, the Stock Analysis package is the one to choose. Before you sign up, though, take a close look at Briefing.com's free service because many investors will find it more than suitable for their needs. By the way, the site offers a free trial of its subscription packages.

BRIEFING.COM AT A GLANCE

Who's It For?
Active investors who want continuously updated daily reports on the markets and stocks of note.

Top Things to Do on This Site:
1. Find trading opportunities by reading the "In Play" feature.
2. Get the lowdown on stocks in the news by reading "Story Stocks."

Don't Miss:
Briefing.com's Learning Center, where you can read clearly written educational material on general investing concepts and more arcane stuff like technical analysis and trading strategies.

LINKS

CBS MarketWatch (cbs.marketwatch.com): An all-purpose market news site aimed at a broader market than Briefing.com. Includes stock research tools, an excellent portfolio tracker, and lots of commentary from investing experts.

IDEAadvisor (www.ideaadvisor.com): Opinionated, expert analysis of stocks making news. Less prolific in its output than Briefing.com.

TheStreet.com (www.thestreet.com): A savvier, more opinionated version of CBS MarketWatch that will appeal to experienced investors.

Canadian Business

www.canadianbusiness.com

What's the Deal?:
Web access to investing articles in one of Canada's top business magazines.

Usefulness Rating: ✓✓

Canadian Content Rating: ✓✓✓✓

Cost: None, unlike the magazine itself.

In the United States, there are numerous glossy magazines that cater to individual investors. In fact, they have a magazine called *Individual Investor* (its Web site is included in this book). In Canada, we have nothing of the kind, really. The closest we come are a number of general purpose business or personal finance magazines that often touch on investing. If investing is your main area of interest, the best of this bunch is *Canadian Business*.

Here's a sample of the investing-related articles I have found on the Web site of *Canadian Business*. One was a piece on TransCanada PipeLines stock. The shares had just come off a nice run-up and readers were warned that slower growth might be ahead. Even so, the article said, TransCanada stands out as a steady dividend play with some long-term growth prospects. Another article zeroed in on Brascan, one of a shrinking number of Canadian conglomerates. Brascan had been on a run-up after years in a coma, but the writer was sceptical. He noted that conglomerates traditionally are priced at a discount to asset values and, moreover, that most such companies usually are a mix of winning and losing component firms.

Canadian Business has also written critically about the surprisingly complex matter of bond commissions. Brokers will tell you that there's no commission charged on bonds, but the fact is that there is a commission built into the price you're paying. You may not see it, the magazine warns, but it's there. Overall, I like the opinionated, prescriptive approach taken by the magazine in its investing coverage. Too much of what you read on financial Web sites is wishy-washy "on this hand, and on the other hand" slush that leaves you rolling your eyes. I have also found this magazine's writers to be knowledgeable and savvy enough to include all sides of the story when highlighting specific stocks.

The Investor 500

For the past couple of years, *Canadian Business* has produced an annual Investor 500 edition that ranks Canada's most valuable companies by one-year return. Lists like this aren't all that helpful to investors because they're backward-looking. In fact, the surest way to lose money this year is to be on last year's high-flyer. That said, the magazine does fill out its Investor 500 issues with reams of helpful stock-picking suggestions. In the past, top stocks in 12 different sectors have been provided, along with lists of what top fund managers were buying. Of course, the whole thing is archived on the Web site. ■

Magazines have a real dilemma on their hands in deciding how much material to provide free on their Web sites and how much to save for people who pay to buy the magazine. I've never done a comparison of what's on the *Canadian Business* site and in the magazine, but there's definitely no sense of stinginess at work. You can see this in the number of articles available online, and in the archive of articles going back a year. To access the archive, use the search engine at the top of the homepage. For Nortel Networks, a company that *Canadian Business* has followed with an aggressively critical eye, I found 80 different articles in the archive.

CANADIAN BUSINESS AT A GLANCE

Who's It For?
Investors seeking opinionated, well-informed articles on stocks, companies, and broader investing issues.

Top Things to Do on This Site:
1. Check the Investing archive for articles published in the current issue, as well as recent issues.
2. Scan the other stories for investing angles.
3. Take a look at the Investor 500, the magazine's annual ranking of companies by their one-year return.

LINKS

MoneySense (www.moneysense.ca): A sister publication to *Canadian Business, MoneySense* is a glossy personal finance magazine that frequently includes articles on stocks and mutual funds.

Individual Investor (www.individualinvestor.com): The Web site of a U.S. investing magazine that can be relied on to provide lots of good stock-picking ideas.

CBS MarketWatch

cbs.marketwatch.com

What's the Deal?:
A top financial Web portal.

Usefulness Rating: ✓✓✓✓

Canadian Content Rating: ✓✓

Cost: Free

I'm reminded of *The Wall Street Journal* when looking at CBC MarketWatch. The king of stock market news sites brings the sort of breadth and authority to the Web that *The Journal* does to print media. In fact, I'd go so far as to say that if you want to find out what's going on in the financial world (U.S. division) at any given moment, this is your site.

I found a good illustration of this one day when the U.S. Federal Reserve had just lowered its trendsetting overnight interest rate by half a percentage point. It happened that the market had been looking for a cut of three-quarters of a point. When the half-point cut was announced, the stock markets tanked. CBS MarketWatch had a great coverage package to keep readers informed. First, there was the main story, headlined "Fed Leaves Street Wanting," then there were sidebars on the Fed's take on the global economy, and on the reaction of the bond market and financial stocks. Rounding out the package were audio reports from MarketWatch correspondents, a chart showing the course of U.S. interest rates over the past few years, and commentary from Irwin Kellner, Marketwatch's chief economist (yes, this is one of very few financial Web sites with its own chief economist), as well as the economist (and writer of thrillers) Paul Erdman.

All of this material was in addition to the regular MarketWatch coverage of the day's top stock stories, developments on global stock markets, and economic and political news. MarketWatch prides itself on its news coverage, with 100 journalists in bureaus located in the United States, Europe, and Asia. The site describes itself as providing "the story behind the numbers," and I think it does.

There's more to MarketWatch than news and analysis, though. You'll also find a stock research centre, a portfolio tracker, a personal finance section, and an online audio/visual archive where you can monitor reports prepared for U.S. radio and television stations. The least interesting section is the one on personal finance. As you would expect, the content is geared to American readers, which means lots of info on IRAs, none on RRSPs.

The MarketWatch site also puts a lot of effort into covering the market for initial public offerings, or IPOs. Planned IPOs are covered, as are the pricing and first day of trading for prominent new issues in the United States, and on global markets. As well, there's quite a decent stock research area that includes a fun-to-use charting feature. Just type in your stock symbol—again, use CA: in front of Canadian symbols—and a one-year chart immediately pops up. What's unique here is that there are buttons that instantly let you change the timeframe or pick a stock index to add to the chart. You can also choose whether to include splits, dividends, and/or earnings announcement dates. The charts are provided by BigCharts, a top-notch charting Web site that is owned by CBS MarketWatch (BigCharts is one of the 50 essential sites in this book).

Tracking Your Portfolio on MarketWatch

There are any number of trackers to be found on the Web, but this one is as good a candidate as any to use for your own personal stock portfolio. One reason is that you can include Canadian stocks—just type a CA: in front of the symbol as in CA:BCE. Another is that this tracker can do tricks you don't often see. My personal favourite is the "allocation" button—click on it and you get a colourful pie graph showing the portion of your portfolio taken up by each stock and fund. The MarketWatch portfolio tracker will also give you all recent news stories for the stocks you own, as well as financial statements and insider trades for U.S. stocks. If you prefer to fine-tune the presentation, just click on "preferences."

The MarketWatch people are apparently so proud of their tracker that they've come up with a feature that causes your personal portfolio to pop up on a separate, small-sized Web page whenever you log into the site. I found this kind of irritating, which is why I availed myself of the "turn off tracker auto launch" button. ▓

Another research feature worth trying is the stock screener. This particular toy is designed to work on a intraday basis, which means it will help find stocks that meet your criteria at any given moment during the trading day. It's actually quite a complex little device, with separate sections for price, volume, fundamentals, and technicals. If you chose technicals, you could look for stocks outperforming or underperforming their 50- or 200-day moving averages, as well as for stocks outperforming or underperforming a set stock index by a percentage supplied by you. With fundamentals, you can select stocks with price-earnings ratios and market capitalization in a range set by you. You can also limit your search to a particular U.S. exchange, but not a Canadian one.

As a top financial Web site, MarketWatch has attracted some serious talent to its stable of writers and columnists. Read through the site on a regular basis and you get a sense the people working there have a mastery of their subject matter. You don't always get this on investing Web sites. Just as important, MarketWatch continually gets top names to write or at least be interviewed. During one particularly rough day for the markets, U.S. index fund pioneer John Bogle did a Q&A session that contained some worthwhile advice. "Times like these are terrible times to make investment decisions," the famed founder of the Vanguard Group said. "To run out and panic and join the crowd is extremely foolish." Another nugget: "[Investors] also should be mentally, psychologically prepared for a 35 to 40 per cent market drop. I've used those numbers in the past and people would kind of ignore them."

Weekends with MarketWatch

Most investing Web sites take the weekend off. Who can blame them? From first thing Monday to late Friday afternoon, they continually churn out market commentary and so forth. It's grueling work that certainly calls for a weekend breather. MarketWatch is different in that it works weekends.

Have a moment for some relaxed Sunday surfing? Try the CBS MarketWatch Weekend package of online video features that you can view on your computer, just as if you were watching television. To find the weekend package, click where it says "MarketWatch TV & Radio." Weekend stories that I caught included an interview with the CEO of online auction company Ebay; an interview on the state of the stock markets with James Grant, editor of *Grant's Interest Rate Observer*; a story on corporate philanthropy; and a look at the potential impact on drug company Eli Lilly when its patent for Prozac ended. ■

MarketWatch is a public company that trades on Nasdaq under the symbol MKTW. It's part-owned by CBS Broadcasting, which explains the extensive use of both audio and video, and the close attention to visuals on the site. The MarketWatch homepage is always loaded to the gills with stories and features, yet it's also cleanly laid out and inviting. If you're unsure of what's available on the site, there's a handy list of the Top 10 features on MarketWatch. This is a great idea that other sites should copy.

CBS MARKETWATCH AT A GLANCE:

Who's It For?
Anyone trying to keep up with and understand what's going on in the financial world.

Top Things to Do on This Site:
1. Keep up on the day's events in the markets.
2. Research or screen stocks.
3. Read the top-flight columnists.

Don't Miss:
The portfolio tracker—it's one of the better ones out there.

Toys:
1. Daily Media Buzz e-mails that list the top investing articles of the day.
2. You can make MarketWatch your homepage.
3. E-mail alerts when companies you're watching make the news, or when a columnist you like files a story to the Web site.

LINKS

Bloomberg.com (www.bloomberg.com): The financial news and data giant's Web site is crisp and functional, but it lacks the pizzazz of CBS MarketWatch.

Briefing.com (www.briefing.com): Similar to TheStreet.com in that it provides opinionated but unbiased market commentary. The presentation is a little rougher, and there's less variety in the stories available.

CNN Money (money.cnn.com): CNN's financial Web site comes across like a slightly lesser version of CBC MarketWatch. Good global business coverage.

TheStreet.com (www.thestreet.com): A savvier, more opinionated version of CBS MarketWatch that will appeal to experienced investors.

ClearStation

www.clearstation.com

Imagine this: You've just set up an account at an online broker, you've got a pile of cash sitting there, and you're ready to trade. Just one problem—what stocks are you going to buy? For answers, let me suggest ClearStation. This is a Web site for active, aggressive investors who want lots of stock-picking ideas, and the means to sift through these ideas to separate the junk from the gems.

Rather than plying you with gimmicky stock-picking strategies, ClearStation employs a down-to-earth three-point approach to picking stocks. The three points are:

• Fundamental analysis, which scrutinizes P/E ratios, PEG ratios, and other aspects of a company's financials.

- Technical analysis, which looks at a stock's price movements to forecast future performance.

- Community, which means consulting other ClearStation users on their thoughts and recommended picks.

   Before we go any further, it needs to be stressed that of all the Web sites in this book, ClearStation is the most demanding in terms of learning to use it properly. You don't just get this site up on your computer screen and intuitively feel your way around to the best tools and features. I point this out not to criticize ClearStation, but to prepare you so you're not deterred by its apparent complexity. This site requires a bit of work on your part, but it's well worth the effort.

   Start by checking out the summary of how the three-point approach works (click on "About Us" at the bottom of the homepage). From there, it's definitely worth clicking on the "Education" link to read the tutorials on how the site works, how to interpret technical analysis graphs, how to use technical analysis, and so on. This all may sound intimidating, but it's not. ClearStation is actually a very democratic site that tries hard to educate newcomers and help them trade effectively.

Signing up for ClearStation

The sign-up process to become a ClearStation member is a model of intelligent, user-friendly design. After you've chosen a username and password, you jump right to a page where you can either create a portfolio or allow ClearStation to get you going with a few stock picks. Then it's over to a watchlist page to set up a group of stocks you want to monitor using the site's resources. From there you'll go to a page that allows you to choose whether to receive e-mail updates when selected ClearStation community members buy, sell, or short stocks. You can also decide whether to receive nightly portfolio updates by e-mail. The final step in the sign-up process gives you the option of going back into the ClearStation site, of taking a tour of the site (strongly recommended), or of heading to an educational area to learn how to use ClearStation's tools. ■

The democratic aspect of ClearStation can best be seen in the "Recommend" area of the site, where you'll find charts showing how the stock picks of site members are doing. One of the charts is called Core and it contains the portfolios of ClearStation's panel of experts. Among them is Kensey, the nom de trade of Douglas Fairclough, the one-time computer programmer who founded ClearStation (he later sold it to E*Trade Group, the online brokerage and bank that is the current owner). Displayed for all to see is the number of recommendations made by Kensey and his colleagues, the percentage of picks that have panned out, and the performance of the portfolio as a whole. Kensey was down for 10 recommendations when I checked in, with 30 per cent of his trades in the black.

If you see an expert who impresses, click on his or her name and you'll be able to view all the stocks in his or her portfolio. Click on a stock symbol and you'll find a quick explanation about why the stock was picked, as well as a series of five technical charts. In addition to the Core stock picks, you'll find a listing of selections by 40 of the most successful ClearStation members. One of the top guns when I checked was someone named Tyrone, who was successful with 67 per cent of his trades.

If you would prefer to generate your own ideas, go to the top of the ClearStation homepage and click on "Tag & Bag." This is a listing of stocks that merit some attention because of fundamental events, technical events, or because they're being recommended by the ClearStation community. Click on a stock symbol in the Tag & Bag area and you'll find a page showing the number of members who have recommended taking long and short positions in the stock (long means playing a stock to increase in price, while shorting is a bet that a stock will fall). You'll also find more technical charts, as well a list of postings to ClearStation's message boards on the stock.

ClearStation Comes to Canada

As this book was being written, ClearStation indicated its intention to cover the Canadian market, as well as other foreign markets. Keep watching. ∎

Although ClearStation is designed to be its own self-contained world of stock research, it's also a good place to research stock ideas you've gleaned from other Web sites. Just type the ticker symbol in the box at the top of the homepage and use the pulldown menu to select a "quote and three-point view." This will take you to a page of charts, message board postings, news headlines, and links to all kinds of prime data.

ClearStation tries to project a friendly image, but my favourite thing about it is the rough-edged, hard-trading demeanour of the community members. These people aren't the b.s.-spouting yahoos you often find on Internet message boards, but rather smart, experienced investors who want to compare notes with like-minded people. If that sounds like you, then learn how to work ClearStation and dive in.

CLEARSTATION AT A GLANCE

Who's It For?
Active traders looking for ideas about stocks to buy and sell.

Top Things to Do on This Site:
1. Find stocks to investigate as possible trading opportunities.

2. Research stock ideas found elsewhere.

3. Read up on how to put technical analysis to work.

Don't Miss:
The e-mail updates sent by ClearStation experts when they make a move in their portfolios.

LINKS

Stockscores (www.stockscores.com): Like ClearStation, this site also teaches the rudiments of technical analysis. Where Stockscores differs is in the way it distills technical indicators into scores that suggest whether a stock is heading higher or lower in the near term.

CNET

www.cnet.com

Lots of financial Web sites can help you follow technology stocks, but how many of them can also help you choose a note-book computer, help you build a Web site, or offer free software downloads? Only CNET, I'd say. Under the CNET banner you'll find a vast network of Web pages that covers the tech world in all its facets. Check out the site map—it's long and detailed enough to be almost ridiculous.

Even with the site map, you'll find that CNET's variety makes it an unruly site to work with. The investing area, called CNET Investor, isn't clearly labelled, which means it's a bit troublesome to locate without help. The thing to do is look on the homepage menu under the heading "Tech News and Investing," and then click where it says "Investor" in tiny print. On the plus side, CNET Investor is a nicely streamlined site that gives you a concise overview of what's happening to tech stocks on a given day.

The highlight on CNET Investor is something called the "Brokerage Center," which is a collection of daily comments from 20 or so top U.S. investment dealers, including Merrill Lynch, Lehman Bros., Goldman Sachs, and J.P. Morgan Securities. Typically, you'll find that each day's comments include brief mentions of a small number of stocks and, in most cases, a "buy," "sell," or "hold" rating, an earnings estimate, and a target price. The Brokerage Center also tracks the stocks that are mentioned most often that day in analyst upgrades, downgrades, rating reiterations, or news coverage. If you simply want to know what stocks have been upgraded or downgraded, there's a link for that as well on CNET Investor.

The CNET Family

CNET.com is owned by Nasdaq-listed CNET Networks, which maintains some 25 Web sites globally, in 18 different languages. Besides CNET.com, the list of CNET properties includes ZDNet (www.zdnet.com), which describes itself as a site for people looking to buy, use, and learn more about technology; mySimon (www.mysimon.com), a comparison shopping Web site; and, CNET Broadcast, which provides tech-focused radio programming in the United States. ■

Another CNET Investor feature to try is its "Momentum Ratings," which are based on the number of "buy," "sell," and "hold" ratings on roughly 4,000 different stocks. Stocks with the most buys and fewest sells and holds over the previous 90 days receive the highest momentum ratings. An explanation of how the methodology for the momentum ratings works declares that a rating of 30 or more means a stock merits a closer look. When I checked the ratings, I found Check Point Software Technology in first, with a rating of 122, followed by Electronic Data Systems at 76, and The Gap at 74. A similar CNET feature to the momentum rating is the

"CEO WealthMeter," a daily tally of how the stock holdings of top tech company executives have fared.

Of course, CNET Investor also offers coverage of the day's top stock stories. These stories are covered in a newsy fashion by in-house writers, with fill-in coverage by Reuters. Unlike TheStreet.com or Briefing.com, CNET doesn't tend to analyse events and deliver a "buy/sell/hold" verdict. CNET Investor also offers a small amount of commentary, but it's not a core strength on this site.

In an effort to differentiate its Web site from some of the others, CNET offers free real-time stock quotes, which is certainly a plus. Delayed quotes are offered as well, along with reasonably useful overviews of U.S.-listed stocks, tech or not. Note that CNET Investor has no data on Canadian-listed stocks, but it does have a good amount of information for Canadian companies listed on U.S. exchanges.

When you're done looking up stocks, don't forget to give the rest of the CNET site a look-see. If you're thinking of buying a computer or related equipment, the site's product ratings are mandatory reading.

CNET AT A GLANCE

Who's It For?
Investors interested in technology and technology stocks.

Top Things to Do on This Site:
1. Read daily analyst commentary in the CNET Brokerage Center.

2. Check the day's top technology stories.

3. Do basic research on U.S.-listed stocks.

Don't Miss:
CNET's momentum ratings, a score based on the number of buy, sell, and hold ratings assigned to a stock by analysts.

Toys:
1. Free real-time stock quotes.

2. A portfolio tracker.

3. Free e-mail newsletters.

LINKS

Briefing.com (www.briefing.com): Provides opinionated, unbiased market commentary on an ongoing basis throughout the trading day. The coverage is very thorough, more so than CNET.

TheStreet.com (www.thestreet.com): Savvy, opinionated market analysis that will appeal especially to experienced investors.

EquityWeb

www.equityweb.com

What's the Deal?:
Expedites your stock research by linking you to more than 150 other investing sites.

Usefulness Rating: ✓✓✓

Canadian Content Rating: ✓

Cost: Free

A special award for simplicity should go to EquityWeb. There's not a Web site mentioned in this book that is easier to use. Here are your instructions. Step One: Type in a stock symbol. Step Two: Click on the "submit" button. Yes, it's that easy. Your pet goldfish can research stocks on the Internet using EquityWeb.

Simple, yes, you might say, but what exactly is this site good for? Actually, it's pretty darn useful if you're researching U.S. stocks or Canadian stocks listed on U.S. exchanges. EquityWeb has assembled roughly 150 links to other investing Web sites. When you submit a stock symbol, you get a page of links that will take you to the exact pages on each of those sites that are relevant to your stock.

EquityWeb was created by stock and option traders who wanted a way to expedite the process of researching stocks on the Internet. "Like many, we too have wasted a lot of time clicking, searching and waiting to obtain valuable information pertaining to our investments," EquityWeb explains on its site. "We know as well as anyone that there is a great deal of information on the Web, it just takes too long to get it. In the time that it takes to search many web sites for related stock information the window of opportunity may have passed."

A cross-section of all the major U.S. investing Web sites is included in the EquityWeb collection of links, including Yahoo Finance, CBS MarketWatch, MSN Money, CNET Investor, Multex Investor, Silicon Investor, and the Motley Fool. There are also more specialized sites such as Clearstation (for technical analysis), Earnings Whispers (for advance buzz on earnings), and Wright Investors' Service (for independent research reports). The sites on EquityWeb won't tell you everything about a stock, but they will give you a one-stop-shopping experience that may well suffice for quick-and-dirty research efforts.

The Bad News about EquityWeb

You know how Web sites are sometimes redesigned in ways that leave you scrambling to find certain things? Well, EquityWeb's collection of links seems to encounter this problem fairly often. When I clicked for a PepsiCo quote on CBS MarketWatch, I ended up on a page detailing some recent enhancements to the MarketWatch site. When I clicked for news from Dow Jones on Pepsico, I found myself on a page from the SmartMoney.com Web site reading "You have requested an invalid page from Smartmoney.com." A few other links left me on a plain blank page.

Keeping all the links shipshape on EquityWeb must be quite a job. Still, you wish they were just a little more diligent at it. ▪

Let's look at a specific example of how you would use EquityWeb. A while ago, I read an article somewhere saying that PepsiCo's share price was close to doing what was once thought impossible —rising higher than the shares of archrival Coca Cola.

That reminded me of how PepsiCo had recently been mentioned on the Multex Investor Web site as one of the most highly recommended stocks by brokerage analysts. I wasn't particularly serious about buying Pepsi shares, just curious. That made for an ideal opportunity to put EquityWeb to work.

After submitting the stock symbol PEP, I went to a links page divided into 12 boxes with the following titles: Quote, Chart, News, Earnings, Filings, Profiles, Financials, Wall Street Recommendations, Ratios and Stats, Insiders, Competitors, and Valuation. Within each box was a choice of between two and 15 different links. In the chart box, for example, there was a link to the BigCharts Web site that showed PepsiCo's share price movement that day in five-minute increments and 15-minute increments. There were other BigCharts links available as well to chart the shares over periods ranging from five days to a decade. Sure, I could have gone to the BigCharts site myself and done these searches, but it would have been a lot more time-consuming than just clicking on the Equity-Web links.

EquityWeb almost never gives you one choice of link in a particular area. For charts, you can use BigCharts or Yahoo Finance or a few others, while the stock quote options include MSN Money, Yahoo, Quote.com, and Quicken.com. There are also a few sites included for option quotes. Most of the other groupings of links offer a similar variety.

The biggest convenience of EquityWeb is that it saves you time mucking around on other Web sites to find the information you need. While it's no sweat finding a quote on Yahoo Finance, it can be time-consuming to scan, say, the FreeEDGAR.com site for regulatory filings on a stock you're researching. Using EquityWeb, it took me just two mouse clicks to get to a five-page list of Pepsico filings going back eight years.

EquityWeb can be useful even if you don't have a particular stock in mind to research. On its rather modest-looking homepage, it has a variety of links under such headings as news, commentary, tech stocks, and miscellaneous links. The links are worth scanning if for no other reason than maybe you'll find a decent financial Web site that you haven't yet seen.

EQUITYWEB AT A GLANCE

Who's It For?

Investors looking for one-stop convenience for stock research.

Top Things to Do on This Site:

1. Research stocks on a variety of Web sites linked to EquityWeb.

2. Check the list of links on the homepage for Web sites you haven't seen before.

LINKS

Investorama (www.investorama.com): Offers a "Best of the Web" directory with more than 16,000 links to sites classified under a variety of investment-related subjects.

Superstar Investor (www.superstarinvestor.com): Includes 20,000 links to top investing Web sites.

FundLibrary.com

www.fundlibrary.com

What's the Deal?:
A top-notch site for researching mutual funds and learning more about investing in general.

Usefulness Rating: ✓✓✓

Canadian Content Rating: ✓✓✓✓✓

Cost: Free

We're a society that loves to get an expert opinion before we buy or consume things. Going to a movie? You might well pick one based on how many stars it got in newspaper reviews. Buying a car? Lots of people use the ratings in *Consumer Reports* and other publications to help them buy. You might not know it, but mutual fund ratings are available as well. If you are trying to find the right fund, they're definitely worth looking at as part of your research.

Finding and then using ratings is a bit of a problem, though. There are close to half a dozen different sources of ratings available in print and on the Internet, and all have their own nuances. Some ratings reflect a fund's long-term performance primarily, while others focus on shorter-term numbers, or on risk-adjusted performance. These differences make it possible for the same fund to get a five-star rating from one outfit and a one-star rating from another. You could avoid all this confusion by simply aggregating all the different views into a single consensus rating, but how would you do that?

There's a simple answer to this question. Just use FundLibrary.com. This Web site will be familiar to many online investors because it was one of the first Web sites in Canada devoted to mutual funds. FundLibrary.com was a leader for a while, but it lost ground to similar sites such as Morningstar.ca and Globefund, both of which have their own proprietary fund rating systems. It's a copycat world, so it wouldn't have been surprising if FundLibrary.com had decided to come up with its own ratings. Luckily it didn't. Instead, it did something a lot more useful by creating a service in which it collects ratings from outside sources and then presents them both individually and combined into a single consensus rating called the FundLibrary.com Composite.

The ratings displayed on FundLibrary.com come from Globefund and Morningstar.ca, as well as from the fund analysis firm Fundata and from Gordon Pape, Canada's original mutual fund guru and author of annual mutual fund rating books. You can quickly find separate listings of the top funds under all four ratings, as well as the Fund Library.com Composite. You can also use a filter to find the funds that get top ratings from some or all raters, or browse through various fund families to see how each individual fund rates. If you do this, you'll quickly notice that the larger fund families have a rough 50-50 split between higher-rated funds and lower-rated funds.

The simplest way to use the various ratings is to look for funds that get top scores all around. To do this, set the ratings filter to give you funds earning five stars from Morningstar and Globefund, an A from Fundata, and four dollar signs from Mr. Pape. If you're a little more flexible, you could adjust the search terms to four or five stars, a B or better, and three or more dollar signs. If you want to simplify things, you could simply go for a list of funds that get top FundLibrary.com composite ratings. When I checked, I found

The Lowdown on FundLibrary.com's Ratings

Here are the five mutual fund ratings you'll find on the FundLibrary.com Web site:

Fundata: Uses letter grades that range from an A for funds with superior past performance to an E for funds with poor performance. The Fundata system equally considers return, risk, and consistency.

Globefund: Uses a five-star system that emphasizes shorter-term results. Funds are rated by having their returns compared on a monthly basis against the yield on ultra-safe 90-day Treasury Bills.

Morningstar.ca: Uses a risk-adjusted five-star system that considers three-, five-, and 10-year performance, with an emphasis on the long term.

Gordon Pape: His ratings start with a single dollar sign, which denotes a fund that is either below average or that offers higher-than-acceptable risk, to four stars, which means a superior fund that should perform among the top 25 per cent of funds in its category.

FundLibrary.com Composite: Combines the previous four ratings into a score out of 100. ■

---

three funds nailed down a perfect 100 in the composite rating: AGF International Value, Altamira Short Term Canadian Income, and National Bank Small Cap. Another 11 funds had composite ratings of 90 or more.

You can also do more sophisticated searches using FundLibrary's filters. For example, you could look for funds that received one star from Globefund and five stars from Morningstar. Presumably, you would get a list of funds that have done well in the long term but have stumbled lately, possibly offering a chance to buy low. If you wanted to emphasize safety in your search, you could keep the same search criteria but also add funds that have a rating of B or higher from Fundata.

If you would prefer to search for funds without using the ratings, then try FundLibrary.com's fund filters (click on "Tools" on the homepage). A fund filter is really a glorified search engine that finds you funds meeting set criteria in areas like management expense ratio or performance over a set period. For example, you might look for Canadian equity funds with MERs below 2.0 per cent and compound average annual returns of 10 per cent or more over 10 years.

Analysis as Well as Numbers

One way FundLibrary.com has differentiated itself from the competition is by providing a lot of expert commentary on funds. Fund analyst Steve Kangas writes a periodic column called Kangas Korner in which he discusses events in the financial markets and the fund industry, and he also offers more informal musing in a feature called Investment Café. For commentary from a stable of investment advisers, head to Advisors Alley. If you would like to read the wisdom of actual fund managers, try Pros Promenade. ■

Once you've found a fund of interest on FundLibrary.com, take a look at the detailed fund profiles the site offers. They're called Fundcards and they'll show you such pertinent information as MER, assets, inception date, and manager. There's also an adjustable performance graph; detailed information on returns over various time periods including calendar years; and a list of the fund's Top 10 holdings. Finally, there's a link to a downloadable brochure for the fund.

Be sure to carefully scan the Fundcards of any funds that score well in the ratings tracked by FundLibrary.com. As useful as these ratings are, they are not sufficient reason unto themselves for buying a fund. While the methodology differs, all ratings are based to a large extent on how funds have done in the past. The inference is that funds that have done well will continue to do so. This does happen sometimes, but if often doesn't. Good funds go into tailspins and bad funds hit lucky streaks—no ratings will warn you that these surprises are ahead. That's the theoretical limitation of ratings. There are several practical ones as well, including the fact that they tell you nothing about things like a fund's investing style, the kind of stocks in its portfolio, or its management expense ratio. You can easily find out this information, but you have to know enough to look for it.

FUNDLIBRARY.COM AT A GLANCE

Who's It For?
Anyone interested in mutual funds.

Top Things to Do on This Site:
1. Check out the outside fund ratings collected by FundLibrary.com and then turned into a single composite rating.
2. Research individual funds, or search for funds that meet your specific investing needs.
3. Read the columns and commentary by fund experts and outside columnists.

Don't Miss:
The Investment Café, which consists of day-to-day musings by fund analyst Steve Kangas.

Toys:
1. An easy-to-use portfolio tracker.
2. E-mailed portfolio updates.
3. A homepage that can be customized.

LINKS

Globefund.com (www.globefund.com): Some of the top fund research tools around, plus access to a vast archive of articles on funds that have appeared in *The Globe and Mail.* As well, Globefund offers a very good portfolio tracker that lets you include both funds and stocks.

FundScope (www.fundscope.com): This independent fund analysis service charges a subscription fee for its fund rating analysis, but it also allows visitors free access to certain services, such as its portfolio risk calculator.

Morningstar.ca (www.morningstar.ca): The Canadian arm of the renowned U.S. fund rater has a first-rate Web site for researching funds. The highlight is the database of Morningstar fund ratings, but there's also lots of fund commentary by in-house analysts and expert guest columnists.

Globefund.com

www.globefund.com

The AIC Advantage Fund is a real piece of work. When it's on a tear, it leaves most other Canadian equity funds in the dust, and when it falters, well, let's just say the results can be ugly. Long term, this fund is so far ahead of the pack that it's almost laughable. According to a fund report I found on Globefund, AIC Advantage had averaged 20.3 per cent annually over the previous 10 years, very close to double the average fund in its class. How many funds did better over that period? None, Globefund showed.

There are three major Web sites for researching mutual funds in Canada and each has its own strengths. One of Globefund's is how quick and easy it is to research any one of the 4,000-plus funds available in Canada. Want an in-depth report on a particular fund?

Just type the fund name into the box at the top of the homepage and you'll jump to a detailed fact sheet that tells you need-to-know information like the management expense ratio, performance over several different time periods, the minimum amount you can invest in the fund, its eligibility for registered retirement accounts, and so on. Want to see how a fund's returns match up against its peers? Then click where it says "Filter" at the top of the homepage and set up a comparison over the past 30 days, 15 years, or anything in between.

Lots of sites offer these sorts of features, but none builds on them the way Globefund does. For example, fund reports on the site contain a link to related *Globe and Mail* stories. I found 537 documents mentioning AIC Advantage, including both full articles and listings of best- and worst-performing funds. Still another example of Globefund's high-quality content can be found in those same fund reports. For all equity funds, there's a list of the Top 10 stocks in the portfolio. Most company names in these lists are linked to profiles and financial statements on Globeinvestor, a sister Web site to Globefund (and another of the 50 essential sites in this book).

To find just the right fund on Globefund, click on the "Filter" button, then use the various pull-down menus to select the search criteria. For the sake of example, you might look for Canadian equity funds with a 10-year average annual return of 10 per cent or more, an MER of less than 2.5 per cent, and a minimum required investment of $500. I found 12 such funds, including AIC Advantage. In all cases, you'll be able to view your search results in seven different ways—standard view, short-term performance, long-term performance, annual returns, quartile rankings, key facts, and five-star ratings.

When using Globefund's Filter function, it's a good idea to take a quick trip through all seven types of reports so that you get the full view of your funds. Here's a good example of what I mean. When I looked at the annual return chart, I found that AIC Advantage lost 12.6 per cent in 1994 and 13.4 per cent in 1999. Those aren't catastrophic losses, especially considering the fact that the

Globefund's Five-Star Rating System

Personally, I think mutual fund ratings are of only limited value. The problem is that they look into a fund's past, then synthesize the results into a rating that investors inevitably use as an indicator of future performance. Often, disappointment ensues. This is no slight on Globefund's ratings, just a general proviso not to put too much stock in anyone's ratings.

Globefund uses a five-star system that emphasizes shorter-term results, a contrast to Morningstar's longer-term view in its own five-star ratings. At Globefund, funds are rated using a process in which returns are compared on a monthly basis with the yield on ultra-safe 90-day Government of Canada treasury bills. Globefund says its historical testing of its rating system has shown that on average, top-rated funds have tended to outperform their peers over a six-month to two-year horizon. ■

fund gained 66.5 per cent in 1996 and then 43.3 per cent in 1997, but I'd be leery of buying AIC Advantage if I were the sort of investor who would be troubled by the possibility of losing 10 per cent or more in a year.

If your search using Globefund's Filter produces a list with dozens or hundreds of funds, you can do a little easy sorting by clicking at the top of a column heading. For example, you might go to the long-term report and click where it says "10 yr." This would shuffle your search results so they ordered from best 10-year numbers to worst. Click on "10 yr" again and the list is reversed so that it runs from worst to best.

By all means take advantage of the content available from *The Globe and Mail* when using Globefund. All you have to do is use the "Article Search" function on the Globefund homepage. I typed "MERs" into the search box and came up with 99 documents, including many of my own Personal Finance columns. A search for "technology funds" produced 172 documents, while a search under "Phillips, Hager & North" produced 119 documents. Another great *Globe* feature that you can access on Globefund is the paper's 15-year mutual fund reviews. These are published twice annually and they include year-by-year performance numbers for all funds sold in Canada. If you're looking for long-term consistency in a fund, this is an essential tool.

GLOBEFUND.COM AT A GLANCE

Who's It For?
Anyone who invests in mutual funds, or wants to.

Top Things to Do on This Site:
1. Search for funds that meet your investing needs.

2. Look up detailed reports on specific funds.

3. Search the database for mutual fund articles from *The Globe and Mail* newspaper.

Don't Miss:
Globefund's coverage of closed end funds (basically mutual funds that are listed on stock exchanges), an obscure but sometimes intriguing investment category.

Toys:
1. A top-notch portfolio tracker (for more details, see the section in this book on Globeinvestor).

2. Monthly e-mail alerts that include news and fund data from *The Globe's* monthly special mutual fund section.

3. Mutual fund Webcasts, which are mutual fund programs from Report on Business Television.

LINKS

FundLibrary.com (www.fundlibrary.com): Fund research tools can be found here as well, but the real attractions are the columns and articles written by in-house and outside experts. FundLibrary.com also has an online discussion forum that covers funds, plus a wide array of other subjects.

FundScope (www.fundscope.com): This independent fund analysis service charges a subscription fee, but it also allows visitors to use certain services, such as its portfolio risk calculator.

Morningstar.ca (www.morningstar.ca): The Canadian arm of the renowned U.S. fund rater has a first-rate Web site for researching funds. The highlight is the database of Morningstar fund ratings, but there's also lots of fund commentary by in-house analysts and expert guest columnists.

Globeinvestor.com

What's the Deal?:
A top site for keeping up with the markets and researching Canadian and U.S. stocks.

Usefulness Rating: ✓✓✓✓

Canadian Content Rating: ✓✓✓✓✓

Cost: Free

Let me be upfront. I work for the *The Globe and Mail* newspaper, which is part of the corporate family that produces Globeinvestor. Not only that, columns and stories I've written are laced throughout the Globeinvestor archive of investing stories. I mention this because I don't want anyone to think I'm doing public relations work by including Globeinvestor in this book. Truth is, I think Globeinvestor is an absolutely essential investing Web site that stands tall on its own merits.

Two things set Globeinvestor apart from the competition. One is the seamless way it treats the Canadian and U.S. stock markets. In fact, this may be the only frontline investing site that covers the Canadian market and Canadian stocks every bit as well as those from the United States. The other Globeinvestor advantage is high-quality news and analysis drawn from *The Globe and Mail*, the globeandmail.com breaking news Web site, ROBTV (a business television channel and another enterprise in the Globe family) and TheStreet.com, a top U.S. investing Web site covered elsewhere in this book. Globeinvestor also offers a top-notch portfolio tracker and other toys. Put it all together and you understand why I feel comfortable praising the site, even while I'm personally associated with it.

Globeinvestor is one of those financial Web sites that you tend to visit often, maybe once a day or more. One reason is that the site offers one of the best market news packages around. On the home-page, you'll find breaking Canadian, U.S., and international financial news from Globeandmail.com, as well as from Reuters. In addition, there are stories from the day's edition of *The Globe* newspaper. Want more? Then click on the ROBTV link for a listing of Webcasts from the day's coverage that you can watch on your computer. For each Webcast, there's a description of the story, the length of the program (usually 10 minutes or less), and a link for either high-speed or low-speed downloading.

Globeinvestor's Quote Pal

Here's a nifty little toy you can use to keep an eye on as many as five stocks or stock indexes during a particular trading day. The Quote Pal is a tiny browser window that shows the latest prices on your chosen stocks (delayed prices are used), along with links for more detailed stock quotes, charts, and news announcements. You can leave the Quote Pal on in the background as long as you want, then collapse it when you're done. ■

Globeinvestor's stocks database is another reason why the site is so handy on a day-to-day basis. In fact, if Canadian investors could have only one site for researching stocks, Globeinvestor would be the hands-down choice. This is not only because of the site's full range of information on both Canadian- and U.S.-listed stocks, but also because of its solid collection of research tools.

You'll find stock quotes, company news and charting, as well as analyst estimates and consensus recommendations. The charting function is versatile in that it allows you to pick a variety of time-frames ranging from intraday to five years, to compare several stocks at once, and to include moving averages, which are an indicator of a stock's price momentum.

Globeinvestor complements its research tools with a "Filter" that you can use to find stocks that meet criteria ranging from price-earnings ratio to one-year share price performance, market capitalization, and price-to-book value ratio. For the Canadian markets, Globeinvestor's filter is one of the best screening tools out there. Unfortunately, this isn't saying much. While most every big U.S. investing site has a solid screening tool to offer, Canadian sites have shown little interest in following suit. Advice For Investors (an essential site covered in this book) has a good screening tool, but you can only use it if you're a paying customer of the site. As for Globeinvestor's filter, I found it to be outclassed by those found on U.S. sites like MSN Money.

The area where Canadian financial Web sites lag behind their U.S. counterparts most egregiously is in analysis and commentary. Globeinvestor is an exception, thanks to its archive of articles that have appeared in the Net Worth section of *The Globe and Mail's* Saturday edition. Scroll down the Globeinvestor homepage and you'll find short descriptions of the latest Net Worth articles, and a link that will take you to the entire story. You can also look at articles going back more than a year. Topics range all over the place, including value investing, labour-sponsored funds, tax tips, the potential impact of mergers on bank stocks, sources of independent stock research, and exchange-traded funds. Complementing the Net Worth articles is a collection of online stock portfolios created by *Globe and Mail* investment reporters to test various theories and strategies for picking stocks. Click on one of the portfolio names and you'll find the latest numbers on how the stocks in it are doing.

Looking for an Online Broker?

The Globe and Mail's annual rating of Canada's online brokers appears in the newspaper each fall, but it's available on Globeinvestor the whole year long. The rating evaluates brokers on such criteria as commission costs, research tools, and Web site usability and speed. The rating is an ideal resource for investors who want to invest online, but are at a loss about which broker to choose. The author is a reliable expert in the field—me. ■

It also has to be noted that Globeinvestor offers one of the better Web portfolio trackers around. The version in use at press time for this book wasn't much to look at, but it did a great job of organizing mutual funds, Canadian stocks, and U.S. stocks into a single portfolio that monitored your returns in all kinds of different ways. For instance, you could look at intraday results, month-to-date and year-to-date results and annual results, among others. A great feature here is the ability to create a line graph showing the performance of your entire portfolio, just the funds, or just the stocks. Of course, each stock and fund is linked to information from either Globeinvestor or its sister site, Globefund. A more informal way to track stocks on Globeinvestor is to use the Stocklist feature. Click on the "Stocklist" button on the homepage and then add the symbols of the stocks you want to track. From there on, all you have to do to get an update on how these stocks are doing is click on the same button.

Note to those concerned about online privacy: The Globeinvestor portfolio tracker is password-protected, while the Stocklist is available to anyone who uses your computer to visit the Globeinvestor site (this is a result of Globeinvestor's use of cookies—for an explanation of what cookies are, see Chapter One). There's no personal information on your Stocklist—you don't enter how many shares you own, or what you paid—but people will be able to view the stocks you're following.

NOTE: As this book went to press, Globeinvestor was set to introduce a premium subscription-based service with commentary, data, and tools not available on the free site.

GLOBEINVESTOR.COM AT A GLANCE

Who's It For?
Investors who wants market news, stock research, and investment commentary and analysis from the pages of *The Globe and Mail's* Report on Business.

Top Things to Do on This Site
1. Keep up with breaking market news from Canada and around the world.

2. Research Canadian and U.S. stocks.

3. Use the portfolio tracker to monitor your investments, or the Stocklist feature to monitor stocks you're just following.

Don't Miss:
The archive of articles from *The Globe's* Saturday Net Worth section.

Toys:
1. A top portfolio tracker.

2. An "express transfer service" that allows you to import stock portfolios from other sites to Globeinvestor.

3. The Quote Pal, a toy for keeping tabs on a few stocks through the trading day.

LINKS

CBS MarketWatch (cbs.marketwatch.com): One of the top U.S. financial Web sites, it's a glossier, more diverse version of Globeinvestor.

IDEAadvisor.com

www.ideaadvisor.com

What's the Deal?:
Highly opinionated, independent research on U.S. stocks.

Usefulness Rating: ✓✓✓

Canadian Content Rating: ✓

Cost: Free basic service; a deluxe package called IDEAtrader is available for paying subscribers.

If brokerage analysts had the freedom to produce research in which they could say anything they wanted about a stock, it's likely their reports would read a lot like the ones found on IDEAadvisor. The in-house analysts working for this site tell it like it is, with no soft-pedalling or equivocating. Here's IDEAadvisor's take on rumours circulating one Friday that Microsoft was about to issue a profit warning. "We believe Microsoft will not warn," analyst Keith C. Applegate wrote. Later in his report he added: "We believe any dip in price is an opportunity to buy into Microsoft shares, and we reiterate our 'Buy' rating, which we upped from 'Hold,' during our fiscal Q3 preview."

Now, this is analysis you can use. Not only is it assertive and informed, it's also independent of any of the potential conflicts that can affect the usefulness of research from brokerage analysts. IDEAadvisor analysts do not own stock in companies they cover, and the firm has no financial ties to any of these companies. The net result is that IDEAadvisor's analysis is as good as the analysts writing it.

So, how good are these guys? The first thing you might want to check is the company they work for, IDEAglobal, a supplier of equity, fixed income, and foreign exchange research to market professionals. IDEAglobal employs about 145 analysts who specialize in such areas as financial, telecom, and healthcare stocks. As for the analysts, the best way to gauge their credibility is to look for the "Analysis" area on the homepage and click on "Browse by analyst." There you'll find links to biographies of all the site's analysts, and their recent research. If you find an interesting report on IDEAadvisor and you're thinking of acting on it, I suggest you check this area first to check up on the analyst involved.

What's Covered on IDEAadvisor?

Technology stocks seem to get the most attention from this site's analysts, although it's just one of the sectors covered, along with health care, Internet, communications, and energy stocks. I checked the "Daily Analysis" area of IDEAadvisor's homepage one particular day and found headlines for stories on Nortel Networks, JDS Uniphase, Adobe, and Celestica (the inclusion of several Canadian companies was a fluke). The only non-tech companies included among the headlines were investment dealer Goldman Sachs and General Electric. ■

Like Briefing.com, IDEAadvisor keeps a tight focus on the stocks in the news on a given day. Go to the homepage and you'll see introductory blurbs on all the companies covered, along with a symbol denoting whether the stock's outlook is up, down, or neutral. The format of the reports is for the analyst to write a short summary of a couple of hundred words that concludes with a mention of how IDEAadvisor rates the company—"buy," "sell," or "hold." At the bottom of each report is a short blurb titled "Market Timing" that gives you a summary of where technical analysts see the stock trading in the near future. Finally, at the bottom of the report, there's a risk tolerance rating for the stock on a scale of five stars, where five is high risk. Microsoft rated four stars.

IDEAadvisor is the sort of Web site that's great to use on a day when a stock you're watching makes the news. You can pretty much depend on IDEAadvisor to interpret the day's events in a context of "to buy, or not to buy." As well, you can tap into the IDEAadvisor database to see what's been written in the past on a stock. I found 30 or so stories going back three months for Microsoft.

IDEAADVISOR AT A GLANCE

Who's It For?
Investors looking for stock analysis by independent experts who aren't afraid to throw their opinions around.

Top Things to Do on This Site:
1. Check for reports on companies in the news that day.
2. Check the archives for previous reports on companies of interest.

Don't Miss:
The bond and currency analysis available on IDEAadvisor—it's not highlighted, but it's there.

Toys:
1. Audio "morning call" programming that allows you to listen as IDEAadvisor analysts talk about the day ahead.
2. A selection of eight e-mail newsletters.
3. Message boards—they're not very busy.

LINKS

Briefing.com (www.briefing.com): Similar to IDEAadvisor in that it provides opinionated, unbiased market commentary. IDEAadvisor tackles fewer stocks in a day, but often provides more detailed research reports.

TheStreet.com (www.thestreet.com): This site is stuffed with analysis of the day's hot stocks, as well as columns on the markets, broad investing issues, and personal finance.

IndexFunds

www.indexfunds.com

What's the Deal?:
A prime source of information on exchange-traded funds, and on the benefits of index investing.

Usefulness Rating: ✓✓✓

Canadian Content Rating: ✓✓

Cost: Free

In the money management business, the most basic test of your ability is to generate investment returns that meet or beat a benchmark stock index. For a manager of a Canadian equity fund, the target is usually the Toronto Stock Exchange 300 composite index; for a U.S. equity fund manager it's the Standard & Poor's 500 index. How well do mutual fund managers actually do against their benchmarks? On average, they don't measure up over the long term.

Here are some numbers. As I was writing this book, Canadian equity funds had returned an average 10.3 per cent over the previous 10 years, while the TSE 300 was up 10.7 per cent. The average U.S. equity fund had an average annual 10-year return of 13.3

per cent, while the S&P 500 was up 18.4 per cent in Canadian dollar terms. Wow, if only you could buy the index. Then you would be well on your way to making higher returns than the average mutual fund.

You can, in fact, buy the index. What's more, an increasing number of people are doing just that through an investment product called an exchange-traded fund, or ETF. An ETF is an index fund, which means it delivers pretty much the same return as the stock index it targets. As you might guess from the name, ETFs are listed on stock exchanges, which means you trade them like stocks. Yes, you'll have to pay brokerage commissions to buy and sell them— think along the lines of $25 to $29 to trade Canadian ETFs at an online broker and the same in U.S. dollars to buy the many ETFs listed on U.S. exchanges.

It's my view that exchange-traded funds could rival the popularity of mutual funds in the years ahead, but for now many investors are baffled by ETFs. While you can look up information on mutual funds in dozens of books and on dozens of Web sites, there are few centralized resources on ETFs that aren't associated either with a company that produces these funds, or a stock exchange that lists them. This is where IndexFunds comes in. If you're looking for independent information to help you choose ETFs, this site should be your first stop.

IndexFunds is a site that covers the entire field of index investing, which means it looks at index mutual funds as well as ETFs. Don't bother with the index fund material—it deals with U.S. index funds and not Canadian ones. It also has to be noted that ETFs are often a better choice than index funds because of their lower ongoing management expenses. In Canada, you can buy a broad-based stock market ETF with a management expense ratio of 0.08 to 0.17 per cent, while index mutual fund MERs can range as high as 1.0 per cent or more. MERs are an especially important factor in index investing because ideally you'll make whatever your target stock index does, minus the fund's MER. Add up the amount you pay in MERs over the years and the total would be significant.

IndexFunds has only a small amount of information on Canadian ETFs, which is unfortunate, because there are a growing number of ETFs listed on the TSE that offer exposure to broad markets, specific sectors, and even Government of Canada bonds. On the other hand, the vast majority of ETFs—close to 100 different funds, to be exact—are listed on the American Stock Exchange, or Amex. These funds cover all the major U.S. stock indexes, as well as broad international indexes, country-specific indexes, and sectoral indexes in areas such as technology, biotechnology, financial stocks, and industrial stocks. The variety, in short, is overwhelming.

Say, for example, that you want a fund to track the broad U.S. market. Will that be an S&P 500 fund, a Wilshire 5000 fund, a Dow Jones U.S. Total Market Index fund, a Russell 1000 fund or, for that matter, a Russell 2000 or Russell 3000 fund? If you like the S&P or Russell funds, would you prefer the original version, or spin-offs that focus only on the value or growth funds in the index? Answers to these questions and more can be found on the IndexFunds site using its "Index Screener."

To find the Index Screener, locate the "Data Central" headline on the IndexFunds homepage and select "Indexes" from the pulldown menu. Then set up a search in which large-cap indexes are ranked by their 15-year returns (that's the longest timeframe available). When I did this search, I found that the Wilshire 5000 index fared best of all broad-based indexes, with an average annual return of 16.5 per cent. Next came the Standard & Poor's MidCap 400 index, at 15.7 per cent, and the S&P 500 at 14.0 per cent.

Once you've found an index you like, go back to the Data Central area of the homepage again and choose "Exchange-Traded Funds" from the pulldown menu. Then have the screener punch up a list of all the large-cap ETFs available. You'll find that you can buy the Wilshire 5000 through Vanguard Total Stock Market VIPERs, and that there's also a S&P MidCap 400 fund and a couple of S&P 500 funds. Click on a fund name and you'll find a page of information that includes MER, top stock holdings, and the overall price-earnings ratio of the stocks in the fund. VIPERs, by the way, are an

ETF product from the U.S. mutual fund giant Vanguard—the acronym stands for Vanguard Participation Equity Receipts.

IndexFunds is full of information on ETF basics as well. Click where it says "ETFzone" on the homepage and you'll find an archive of articles under such headings as "ETF Basics and How to Use Them" and "Canadian-Based," which contains a few articles by Canadian mutual fund analyst Dan Hallett about the ETF scene north of the border. The ETFzone is also a good place to go to keep up with the latest ETF news developments and, believe me, there are new developments all the time. When I took a peek at the site, Barclays Global Investors, a major North American ETF player, had just released three new technology index funds. As well, there had been a recent announcement of a new China ETF that would be listed on the New York Stock Exchange.

Even with all the help IndexFunds offers on making sense of ETFs, you may still find yourself overwhelmed by the variety. If this is the case, then take a look at the list of the site's favourite ETFs (you'll find the list in the ETFzone). The top three favourites when I checked were the Vanguard total stock market fund, followed by the iShares Russell 3000 Fund, and the iShares Dow Jones U.S. Total Market Index Fund. As well, the IndexFunds homepage has a list of the most popular ETFs by assets. If you want to see what other investors have to say about ETFs, then click on the "Discuss" button on the homepage for the IndexFunds message boards.

If you're sceptical about index investing, try reading some of the articles in the "Learn" area of the IndexFunds site. If you're still doubtful afterwards, by all means try to find some traditional mutual funds that will outperform the major stock indexes in the years ahead. Good luck. Unless you're a fund-picking genius, it won't be easy.

INDEXFUNDS AT A GLANCE

Who's It For?
Investors looking for help in choosing exchange-traded funds, as well as anyone who wants the lowdown on index investing.

Top Things to Do on This Site:

1. Read the news stories on the latest developments in the ETF world.

2. Compare the performance of various stock indexes to help you select the best ETFs.

3. Read the detailed ETF profiles.

Don't Miss:

The "Learn" area of the site—it's full of articles that will appeal to both indexing novices and veterans.

LINKS

The American Stock Exchange (www.amex.com): The Amex is where most U.S. exchange-traded funds are listed. Click where it says "Exchange Traded Funds" on the homepage and you'll find detailed information on each fund.

Individual Investor

www.individualinvestor.com

What's the Deal?:
This site is overflowing with stock-picking ideas.

Usefulness Rating: ✓✓✓

Canadian Content Rating: ✓

Cost: Free

In the world of investing magazines, *Individual Investor* is an also-ran. At the magazine stores I frequent, *Individual Investor* is always relegated to the lower or back shelf, while *Fortune*, *Forbes,* and *Smart Money* get the primetime space at eye level. *Individual Investor* is actually a pretty fair magazine, but it's a better Web site.

Here's why. While many investing Web sites focus their analysis and commentary on the stocks that make the news each day, Individual Investor takes a more enterprising approach. Often, the analysts who work for the Web site will run their own screens to search for stocks that meet particular criteria. Other times, the site's columnists will highlight a particular stock, or riff on a stock-picking idea of their own. There are also longer analytical stories that tackle subjects like the 50 technology stocks poised for long-term gains. The overall feeling the site provides is one of reflection rather than knee-jerk reaction to whatever the markets are doing.

A typical Individual Investor feature is "Stock of the Day," which you'll find on the homepage. Stocks are selected for inclusion for various reasons, maybe because they're hot at the moment, because they've been overlooked, or because they have been growth machines over a long period. Strangely, I found several Canadian stocks listed in the Stock of the Day archive, including Placer-Dome, Nova Chemicals, and Alcan. Stocks mentioned in the archive have the current price noted, as well as the price when they were recommended. Individual Investor deserves kudos for making itself accountable like this.

The Magic 25

Every year, *Individual Investor* picks a portfolio of 25 stocks that promise great things. All right, so does every other investing magazine. The difference with *Individual Investor* is that the Magic 25 is front and centre on the magazine's Web site so that readers can check the progress of each stock, and refer back to the magazine's rationale for picking the company in the first place.

In regular updates, *Individual Investor* analysts assign buy, hold, and sell ratings to Magic 25 stocks. A buy means there's still room for the stock to run, a hold means it's worth hanging onto the stock but probably not a good idea to buy more, and a sell means it's either time to lock in profits or jettison a bad pick.

Magic 25 companies are divided into a few different categories, such as hidden gems, high fliers, titans, and bargain buys. The long-term track record for Magic 25 portfolios is pretty impressive. Since 1992, they have outperformed both the S&P 500 and Nasdaq by a wide margin. ■

For more stock ideas, check the "Commentary" and "Analysis" areas of the Individual Investor Web site. A Commentary feature I found was a column on so-called anti-hero stocks, which are basically old economy stalwarts. Under Analysis, I found a transcript of an online discussion forum in which Individual Investor analysts took questions from readers. Most of the questions were along the lines of "What do you think or this or that stock...?"

Individual Investor runs an online discussion forum and promotes the service aggressively by listing the Top 10 forums of the day on the homepage. There's also a set of stock research tools provided by an outside Web site called ShortInterest.com. There's some unique stuff here, so definitely give it a look. For example, you'll find tables showing the companies that have attracted the greatest amount of short interest, or in other words, the companies that investors are most pessimistic about.

New material appears often enough on Individual Investor to make the site worth visiting a few times a week. If you stop by less often, visit the site's archives for a day-by-day listing of what you missed. Like any good investing Web site, Individual Investor also lets you type in a stock symbol to see if a company has been mentioned in past articles.

INDIVIDUAL INVESTOR AT A GLANCE

Who's It For?
Investors seeking investing ideas that aren't necessarily based on the hot stocks of the day.

Top Things to Do on This Site:
1. Scan the homepage for the latest articles and columns.
2. Read the Stock of the Day feature.
3. Check the Magic 25 portfolio, which consists of Individual Investor's top stock picks for the year.

Don't Miss:
Investor University, which consists of clear, readable tutorials on investing subjects ranging from buying stocks on margin to how to interpret a company's cashflow numbers. To find Investor University, click on the "Education" button on the homepage.

LINKS

MSN Money (moneycentral.msn.com): A slick, fun-to-use site offering top stock research and screening tools, as well as commentary from some of the Web's best investing columnists.

TheStreet.com (www.thestreet.com): Analysis of the day's trading action plus lots of other investing stories. Whereas Individual Investor caters to a broad range of investors, TheStreet.com is primarily for savvy types who do a lot of trading.

Canadian Business (www.canadianbusiness.com): Investing articles from this magazine can be found online. Unlike Individual Investor, there's no content provided especially for the Web site.

Investing:Canada

What's the Deal?:
A guided tour through some great Canadian online investing resources.

Usefulness Rating: ✓✓✓✓

Canadian Content Rating: ✓✓✓✓✓

Cost: Free

Real estate investment trusts were on the minds of a lot of investors the last time the stock markets tumbled. No wonder. Though conservative compared to common stocks, REITs are plenty attractive in a bear market because of their potential to provide steady income and modest capital gains. Ordinarily, REITs don't get much attention other than from a minority of brokers and investors who like them as a way of adding a bit of zip to the income portion of a portfolio. When REITs suddenly became popular, many people were at a loss as to where to go to learn more about them.

A REIT, for those who don't know, is a stock-like security that pays regular distributions to investors based on the profits generated by a portfolio of real estate holdings after expenses are paid. REITs are actually a sub-category of income trusts, which can be based on businesses ranging from oil wells to hydroelectric generation to sugar refining.

As popular as income trusts were, I had not been able to come up with a decent answer when readers asked me for suggestions on how to research them. Sure, I could have directed people to a Web site like Globeinvestor, but then you would have to know the stock symbol of the REIT in order to look it up. The trick was to find a site that listed all the REITs available, as well as pertinent facts about each. After much searching, I finally found the motherlode of information about REITs on Investing:Canada.

Investing:Canada is an independent site that was once a part of About.com, a network of several hundred Web sites, each covering a specific subject and each tended by a "guide" who is an expert in the field. The guide for Investing:Canada is Marco den Ouden, who works in television news in British Columbia. Mr. den Ouden doesn't have any formal investing credentials, other than four years spent pursuing a Bachelor of Commerce degree at McGill University. This strikes me as a plus in that he's not beholden to one particular philosophy or vested interest.

The Investing:Canada Manifesto

"My objective with this site is to provide a useful and informative resource for Canadian investors. If you're not sure where to find certain Canadian investment information on the Internet, check my site or email me. If it exists, I'll find it!" ∎

—Marco den Ouden, as quoted in his Web site biography

REITs represent only a tiny fraction of the topics covered on Investing:Canada. There are broad subjects like RRSPs, mutual funds, and brokers, and more specific ones like ethical investing, earnings reports, insider trading, and income trusts. When you find a topic of interest, click on it and you'll jump to a page of links edited by Mr. den Ouden. Some links will be to other Web sites, while others are to articles, charts, and graphs.

To get the lowdown on REITs, I clicked where it said "Special-ized Investing" on the homepage and found a link to the holy REIT grail—a table of all trusts traded on the Toronto Stock Exchange, including the stock symbol, frequency of cash distributions, amount of the distribution, market price, and yield. There was a similar chart for oil and gas trusts, as well as several articles to read. The appeal of a site like Investing:Canada is that it's laced with links. For each income trust listed in the tables I found, there was a link to a corporate profile page that itself included links to infor-mation on several other investing Web sites. For example, there were links to online stock discussion forums on Stockhouse Canada, regulatory filings on SEDAR (stands for System for Elec-tronic Document Analysis and Retrieval), and financial reports from Globeinvestor.

Spend some time browsing through Investing:Canada to find what's useful to you. I did and I found several sites and resources that I hadn't come across on my own. I also found a few clunkers —links to sites that were dormant, irrelevant, or second-rate, and to articles that were two and three years old. Also, the REIT chart mentioned earlier contained a small amount of information that was outdated by several months. These quibbles are minor, though. Mainly, I think Investing:Canada is a must-see resource for investors looking for a Canadian slant on all things financial.

INVESTING:CANADA AT A GLANCE

Who's It For?
Investors looking for suggestions on worthwhile investing Web sites and resources.

Top Things to Do on This Site:
1. Check for topics of interest and then browse the links provided.
2. Read the market coverage, including the relative strength tables that show the top-performing stocks on the Toronto Stock Exchange.

Don't Miss:
The profiles of investing newsletters.

LINKS

Investorama (www.investorama.com): This education-oriented investing Web site includes a "best of the financial Web" directory of Web sites.

EquityWeb (www.equityweb.com): A stock research Web site that works by pulling in bits of information from dozens of linked sites, including most of the biggies.

InvestinginBonds.com

www.investinginbonds.com

What's the Deal?:
Solid, basic information on the bond market

Usefulness Rating: ✓

Canadian Content Rating: None

Cost: Free

The bond market is a fair bit larger than the stock market, but coverage of the stock market utterly eclipses that of the bond market. That's as it should be. Bonds may finance the activities of governments and corporations the world over, but they're dead boring for the most part. Sure, bond prices move up and down, but there's none of the drama of the stock market. No price spikes up or down, no doubling your money or losing your shirt.

This, of course, is why we buy bonds. They add a nice, safe core to an investment portfolio. Come to think of it, how do you buy a bond? What should you look out for? What are the key issues? A checklist would certainly be useful here, and that's why

Investing in Bonds is included in this book. This is not a great Web site for Canadian investors, as you'll quickly notice when you look at the site. Much of the material is aimed at the U.S. bond market, where municipal bonds play a huge role, unlike in Canada. Also, whereas Canadian investors would want to know about Government of Canada bonds, the Investing in Bonds Web site looks at U.S. Treasuries.

Still, there's some useful content on this Web site that you really should read if you want a primer on how the bond market works. Start by scrolling down the homepage to where it says "Getting Started: Educate Yourself About Investing in Bonds!" There are seven steps here, the first being to read a very basic overview of what bonds are all about. How basic? Try this opening line on for size: "A bond is a debt security, similar to an IOU." That simple enough for you?

Next, there's a checklist that is designed to provide you with a list of questions to ask yourself before buying bonds. There are places to fill in a sort of questionnaire about your investing needs, and an accompanying "perspectives" blurb to explain the various options. For instance, there's a section dealing with how much risk you're willing to accept. The questionnaire offers three choices (very little risk, modest risk, and substantial risk), while the blurb tells you about how credit quality influences both the interest payout and riskiness of bonds. The lower the credit quality, the less safe a bond is, and the more it has to offer in yield to entice investors to buy it.

Most of the other parts of "Getting Started…" are worth reading as well, especially a section dealing with how much of your portfolio to invest in bonds. Once you're done, move on and check out the explanation of how zero-coupon bonds work. Often called strip bonds, zero coupons are an ideal way to add a fixed-income component to your registered retirement savings plan. Other topics worth exploring include corporate bonds and high-yield bonds, also called junk bonds. There's also a glossary that offers nicely boiled down explanations to help you understand things like the difference between yield, yield curve, yield spread, and yield to maturity.

INVESTINGINBONDS.COM AT A GLANCE

Who's It For?
Anyone who wants to build an understanding of how to buy bonds and how the bond market works.

Top Thing to Do on This Site:
Browse your way through the educational material.

Don't Miss:
"Where Wall Street Meets Main Street," a simple, bordering on simplistic, answer to the question, Why should I care about the bond market?

LINKS

Bloomberg.com (www.bloomberg.com): The financial news and data company's Web site includes bond quotes for U.S. Treasuries, Government of Canada bonds, and other global issues.

Briefing.com (www.briefing.com): This top site for monitoring the day's hot stocks includes bond coverage as well.

DBRS.com (www.dbrs.com): This is the Web site of the Dominion Bond Rating Service, which is a major bond rater in Canada. The site is mainly for paying subscribers, but it does offer some general information on how ratings work, as well as a limited number of actual ratings updates.

Investopedia.com

www.investopedia.com

What's the Deal?:
An ideal place to go when you don't understand an investing term or concept.

Usefulness Rating: ✓✓✓✓

Canadian Content Rating: Not applicable

Cost: Free

Sometimes, even experts need help with investing terms. Take me, for example. While researching a column a while ago on finding free real-time stock quotes, I came across a service called FreeRealTime.com that offers a nicely detailed real-time quote at no charge. Maybe too detailed. Among the pieces of information offered in the quote was something called VWAP. At the risk of embarrassing myself, I have to say that I didn't have a clue what VWAP was. To me, it sounded like something my boys yell at each other while running through the house playing superheroes.

VWAP, I found out, means volume weighted average price. VWAP is a measure that pension funds sometimes use to evaluate the quality of stock trades. It's calculated by totalling the dollars traded for every transaction (price times shares traded) involving a particular stock and then dividing by the total number of shares traded in a day. A good buy trade would be one where the price is lower than the VWAP, while a good sell trade would be one where the price is higher than the VWAP. I learned all of this from Investopedia.com, a Web site I often turn to in those humbling moments when I run smack into an investing term I don't understand.

Trust me, once you know about Investopedia.com, you'll often find yourself shuttling between it and other investing sites as you uncover new terms and seek easy-to-understand definitions. To show you what I mean, let's go back to FreeRealTime.com and look up a real-time quote. Right away, you're going to start running into technical terms that you may not understand. For example, there are the bid and ask prices. This is basic stuff, but novice investors are sometimes confused by these terms. If that's you, just type "bid price" into the search box at the top of the Investopedia homepage. The definition provided: "The price a buyer is willing to pay for a stock."

FreeRealTime.com quotes also tell you the bid size. If you were to jump over to Investopedia and search for a definition, you would find that bid size is "The number of shares a buyer is willing to pay for the quoted bid price." Want more information? Often, Investopedia provides a link to articles from other Web sites that offer extra information. The definition of bid price included a link to a useful article titled "Trading—Bid, Ask, and Spread." Of course, there's also the dreaded VWAP to contend with on FreeRealTime.com. If the definition provided doesn't cut it, try the linked explanatory article titled: "Volume Weighted Average Price: Evaluation or Evasion?"

Investopedia.com is the work of a pair of Edmonton residents, Cory Janssen and Cory Wagner, who on the site go by the name the Investing Guys. They say the point of the site is to make investing less intimidating and to help people more effectively manage their own money. No question, the site delivers easy-to-understand explanations that, unlike some other sources of information, don't leave you only half as puzzled as you were before.

Yes, But What Does It *Really* Mean?

Investopedia's definitions don't just give you a technical definition—they also tell you what a word or phrase means in practical terms. Here's an example from the site's definition of a **stop-loss order**:

What Does It Mean?: An order placed with a broker to buy or sell when a certain price is reached. It is designed to limit an investor's loss on a security position, sometimes called stop market order.

Investing Guys Say: Set a stop loss order for 10 per cent below what you bought the stock for and you will limit your loss to 10 per cent. Stop-loss orders are certainly an undiscovered gem in the investing world. It's also a great idea to use a stop-loss order before you leave for holidays or enter a situation where you will be unable to watch your stocks for an extended period of time. Note: Many online brokerages won't place a stop-loss unless you phone them. ■

You can use Investopedia.com as an online investing dictionary, or you can browse the site to see what looks interesting. Start with the list of the Top Five terms people are looking up on the site. The list of terms that I found was: EBITDA, CAGR, P/E Ratio, Bo Derek, and GAAP (let's leave it to Investopedia.com to explain these terms). You can also look up phrases and terms under such categories as bonds, buzz words, fundamental analysis, mutual funds, and stock trading.

Investopedia.com also offers tutorials on topics that are divided into three groups—basic, more advanced, and active trading. The basic tutorials are a perfect place to go if you have questions that run as basic as what stocks are, and why stock prices change. Among the more advanced topics are reports on buying on margin, short selling, technical analysis, risk management and diversification. The active trading section covers things like advanced trading strategies.

There's another section of Investopedia.com called "Articles & Insight." It's a hit-or-miss series of articles by the Investing Guys themselves and other experts on topics ranging from the importance of order execution when buying stocks to reading financial statements and keeping emotions out of your investing decisions. Think of it as good browsing fodder for a moment when you feel like adding to your investment knowledge base.

INVESTOPEDIA.COM AT A GLANCE

Who's It For?
People looking for simple but not simplistic definitions of investing terms, and for topical education material on investing.

Top Things to Do on This Site:
1. Use the online investing dictionary.
2. See what terms other investors have been looking up.
3. Read the tutorials and articles on a wide range of investing subjects.

Don't Miss:
The free weekly e-mail newsletter that includes a term of the week, newly added terms on the Investopedia.com site, and a tutorial on an investing topic.

LINKS

Investor Learning Centre (www.investorlearning.ca): A non-profit agency that provides investment education for Canadians. The Web site is full of easy-to-understand investing primers on all kinds of investing subjects.

InvestorCanada

What's the Deal?:
Read or listen to mutual fund managers talking about their favourite stock picks.

Usefulness Rating: ✓✓✓

Canadian Content Rating: ✓✓✓✓✓

Cost: Free

Mutual fund managers are an overlooked source of investing wisdom. While investors and the financial media hang off of every little utterance from brokerage analysts, fund managers are consulted infrequently. It's too bad, because you can make an argument that the people who run mutual fund portfolios are a better source of information on stocks.

Fund managers and their staff sift through hundreds of companies to find the right stocks for their portfolios. When they find something good, they put their money where their mouth is by purchasing the stock. From there, these managers watch the stock intently, maybe buying more when the price falls and unloading the whole position when it reaches a certain price target, or if the company's prospects change. In addition to their familiarity with the stocks they choose, fund managers have a greater degree of freedom than analysts to discuss them intelligently. Analysts have to be ever-wary of annoying the companies they cover for fear that these firms will go elsewhere for fee-generating advisery services. When I was an investment reporter at *The Globe and Mail*, I occasionally spoke with fund managers for daily stock market stories and I almost always thought I got good-quality insight.

If you want to hear what fund managers say about the stocks they've bought for their portfolios, go to InvestorCanada. This extremely well-executed Web site interviews managers several times a week and then stores the conversations online as an audio file you can listen to with a RealPlayer. There are also written transcripts, which I happen to find a lot more useful, as well as quick summaries of the points raised by the interview subjects.

Head to the InvestorCanada homepage and you'll find blurbs for five or so interviews, along with a notation of the stocks discussed. You'll also find a partial transcript of the latest interview. Some of the managers I found on the sight included Veronika Hirsch, who talked about gold stocks, particularly Teck and Placer Dome; Fred Pynn of Franklin Templeton, who talked about the growth at a reasonable price—GARP—school of investing and how it applies to T-shirt maker Gildan Activewear; and Jeff Busby of AGF, who talked about value investing and Xerox.

If you're mainly curious to see which stocks are being discussed on the site, click on "HotStocks" for a list of the companies mentioned in the previous 10 interviews. For each stock, there's the current price, the price at which it was suggested, and the percentage change (note that dividends and stock splits are not factored in), as well as the name and firm of the manager who suggested it.

Top Picks

Go to the "HotStocks" area of InvestorCanada and you will be able to view the most successful recent stock picks by fund managers and analysts who have been interviewed on the site. Here are some top picks I found:

- Lafarge, up 179.8% (suggested by Tom MacLaren, Clarington Funds)
- eBay, up 110.6% (suggested by Ian Ainsworth, Altamira)
- Magna International, up 108.9% (suggested by Martin Gerber, Ethical Funds)
- Franco-Nevada Mining, up 100.6% (suggested by John Embry, Royal Bank Financial Group)
- Harrowston, up 88.5% (suggested by Keith Graham, AIM/Trimark Funds)
- Stantec, up 71.8% (suggested by John Sartz, Global Strategy)
- Kingsway Financial Services, up 75.5% (suggested by Richard Fogler, Kingwest and Co.)
- Primex Forest Products, up 71.3% (suggested by Robert Tattersall, Saxon Mutual Funds) ∎

Click on the manager's name in the HotStocks area and you'll jump to a summary of the interview and, if you want, a link to the full interview as well. If you click on the stock's name, you'll find a short description of the company as well as a summary of what the stock has done over the past year. Also available in the Hot-Stocks area is a list of all stocks suggested over the previous few years (click on the "All" button). InvestorCanada also chats with economists, the occasional brokerage analyst, financial advisers, fund industry executives, and corporate executives. I found interviews with the chief executive officers from such companies as Nova Chemicals, Fortis, Sandisk, Intrawest, and TransAlta.

All in all, InvestorCanada offers a truly useful service that you'll turn to often. My one quibble was that the site needed a search function capable of locating references to specific stocks or investing subjects. However, I was told that InvestorCanada planned to add a sophisticated search engine that would permit users to comb through the archives using criteria like, say, "stocks that top-down oriented European fund managers have picked." Great idea.

INVESTORCANADA AT A GLANCE

Who's It For?
People interested in tapping into the stock-picking wisdom of mutual fund managers.

Top Things to Do on This Site:
1. Troll for investing ideas by checking to see the stocks mentioned in the latest manager interviews.
2. Hear corporate executives talk about their companies.

Don't Miss:
The "HotStocks" archive, which lists all stock suggestions made on InvestorCanada recently and in the past.

Toys:
1. Daily and weekly e-mail newsletters.
2. An investing glossary.

LINKS

Q1234.com (q1234.com): The sister Web site of InvestorCanada, Q1234.com provides an audio archive of quarterly earnings reports, special announcements, and annual meetings of a good cross-section of publicly traded Canadian companies, including Inco, Dorel, Rogers Communications, Aliant, and SR Telecom.

BestCalls (www.bestcalls.com): You'll find a schedule of upcoming conference calls for major U.S. companies here. Some calls that have already taken place are archived as audio files on the site, while recordings of other calls are available if you call a toll-free telephone number.

Investor Learning Centre of Canada

www.investorlearning.ca

What's the Deal?:
An ideal place for Canadians to go for help with investing basics.

Usefulness Rating: ✓✓✓

Canadian Content Rating: ✓✓✓✓✓

Cost: Material on the web site is free; the ILC publishes a variety of books and charges for them.

Few things in the investing world are as outwardly simple and inwardly complex as bonds. Most investors know at least in broad terms what bonds are and why they are essential for a serious portfolio. But ask them to explain how bonds work in any detail and it's a different story. What's yield to maturity? What's par value? How do strip bonds work? Now we're getting a little more complicated. It's all the more difficult to master the subject of bonds because there's so little information out there to explain the necessary concepts in a simple way. Most sources will give you definitions full of technical terms that themselves require definitions.

It's for this reason that I like the Investor Learning Centre's Web site. When you have a question about investing, this is an ideal place to start your search for answers. To learn more about bonds, look under the "Money School" heading on the ILC homepage and click on "Investment Sector." You'll then jump to an online learning package that includes a module on the government and corporate bond markets. Among the subjects covered are how you can make capital gains on a bond, why some bonds trade for more than their face value and some for less, how to pick the right bond, and how the bond market operates. Want something a little more succinct, say a simple definition of the term *yield* or *par value*? Then look under "Money School" again for the online glossary. Just type in the term you want defined and click where it says "Go."

What Is the Investor Learning Centre?

The ILC is an independent, non-profit group created by the Canadian Securities Institute, which is the organization that administers educational programs in the investment industry. In addition to its Web site, the ILC maintains walk-in resource centres in Toronto, Edmonton, and Calgary.

The ILC also runs seminars, and publishes a series of investing books that are well worth reading. A great starter book for people interested in investing is the ILC's *How to Invest in Canadian Securities*. To order ILC books or find out about seminars in your area, call 1-888-452-5566. ∎

Another way to tap into the information on the ILC Web site is to look at the list of frequently asked investing questions—to find the list, look under "Question of the Week." I found 137 questions answered, covering such diverse issues as the definition of large-, medium- and small-capitalization stocks, how short-selling works, and why the unit price of a mutual fund falls after a distribution. Also, be sure to scan the list of subjects covered in the "Focus On" area of the "Money School" page. For all the subjects listed here— the ones I found ranged from bear markets to analyst reports and technical analysis—you'll find a list of suggested books and Web sites that will help you learn more.

INVESTOR LEARNING CENTRE OF CANADA AT A GLANCE

Who's It For?
Anyone with a question related to investing.

Top Things to Do on This Site
1. Check out the online educational material.

2. Find books and Web sites related to investing issues of interest to you.

3. Use the online glossary.

Don't Miss:
The online investing quizzes. You'll find them under the "Money School" heading on the homepage.

LINKS

Investopedia.com (www.investopedia.com): A thorough, fun-to-use encyclopedia of investing terms. Educational Web sites don't come any better, at least in the investing realm.

Morningstar.ca

www.morningstar.ca

What's the Deal?:
One of Canada's best mutual fund Web sites.

Usefulness Rating: ✓✓✓✓

Canadian Content Rating: ✓✓✓✓✓

The Templeton Growth Fund is Canada's largest mutual fund, and one of its oldest funds as well. You'd think these facts would entitle the fund to some patience and understanding when it hits a rough patch, but apparently not. After a disastrous performance in 1998, sentiment turned decisively against Templeton Growth. Financial advisers, who once regarded the fund as almost an automatic choice for their clients, lost faith. Many investors cashed out, and fund analysts began to highlight other global equity funds as a better choice.

The storm passed, as storms usually do when they hit blue-chip mutual funds, and gradually the "what's wrong with Templeton

Growth?" chatter abated. Now, say you were an investor looking for a conservative global equity fund. Templeton Growth would naturally come to mind, but you would probably be cautious because of its recent history. What's called for in this situation is some expert analysis that would provide some guidance on whether or not to buy Templeton Growth.

I now direct your attention to Morningstar.ca, the Canadian online arm of Chicago-based Morningstar Inc. Morningstar is to fund-rating as the New York Yankees are to baseball. In other words, they rule. Calling up a profile of Templeton Growth on Morningstar.ca was simple—I just typed the fund name into the search box on the homepage. From there, I jumped to a Morningstar Quicktake Report that sliced and diced the fund in almost every conceivable way. The wealth of facts and figures was impressive, but what really stood out was a report by a Morningstar analyst on Templeton Growth.

This is an important point, so pay attention. Other mutual fund Web sites will shower you with data about funds, but they generally lack specific analysis about individual funds. Morningstar.ca gives you both the numbers, and expert interpretation of their meaning. The report on Templeton Growth was headlined "Has this behemoth value-style fund finally turned the corner?" Now, that's the heart of the matter. The report's conclusion was that Templeton Growth had indeed turned things around, yet questions lingered about whether this success could be sustained. All in all, you would call the Morningstar outlook cautiously optimistic.

Morningstar is most famous for its fund rating system, which works on a scale of five stars. In the United States, Morningstar fund ratings are avidly watched and a five-star score is sometimes said to be a virtual guarantee of investor interest. Like most ratings, Morningstar's are better at sizing up past developments than predicting future performance. Still, the Morningstar style of fund rating is scientific enough to be a reasonably credible indicator of fund quality.

Each individual fund rating is the end product of an analysis that rewards funds able to produce both strong performance and low risk. In terms of performance, funds are rated on their three-,

Stocks Are Covered, Too

As you'll see when you read about Morningstar.com, the next Web site covered in this book, the U.S. arm of Morningstar provides some excellent analysis of stocks as well as mutual funds. The Canadian site is gradually getting into stock analysis, too. Click on the "Stocks" button on the Morningstar.ca homepage and you'll find profiles of Canadian stocks written by in-house analysts, as well as reports on some U.S. stocks.

The Canadian reports are descriptive more than analytical, but they do provide some interesting insights through their listing of mutual fund manager activity in a stock. You'll see the extent to which fund managers are buying the stock, as well as holding their position, selling some shares or closing out their position altogether. ■

five-, and 10-year returns. Funds that have been around for five or more years always have their long-term numbers emphasized more than their short-term record. In assessing risk, Morningstar looks not only at losses but also periods when a fund underperforms treasury bills. The idea here is to penalize funds that make money but can't match the returns of a risk-free investment like a T-Bill.

The next step in the analysis is to subtract the risk score from the return score. The resulting number is then used to rank all funds within a category. Five-star funds are considered to be those in the top 10 per cent of the rankings, while four-star funds are in the next 22.5 per cent, three-star funds in the next 35 per cent, and two-star funds in the next 22.5 per cent. The bottom 10 per cent get just a single star. This method of apportioning stars sounds a little arcane, but it serves a purpose. Only outstanding funds get a five-star rating, while only the truly putrid get a single star. The vast majority of funds end up where they belong, in the mediocre middle. Templeton Growth, by the way, nailed a four-star rating.

Besides its star ratings Morningstar.ca offers a tonne of insightful, nicely displayed content to help you choose a mutual fund and learn more about investing in general. Be sure to check the homepage for fund and fund industry commentary from Morningstar analysts and outside contributors. Then, try the "Fund Focus" feature, which includes the latest analytical fund reports issued by Morningstar's staff.

Of course, Morningstar.ca also works well if you want a fund for your portfolio, but don't have a clue about which one. Here are a couple of different approaches:

- Five-Star Funds: There's a link on the Morningstar homepage to a list of five-star funds. When I checked, there were 80 funds of all types listed in alphabetical order. Each fund entry on the list is linked to a full Morningstar profile. As well, all funds appear on the list with their quartile performance over one-, three-, and five-year periods. Quartiles, by the way, are simply a way of breaking all funds into four groups according to their returns over a set timeframe. The best 25 per cent are called "top quartile" and so on.

- Top Performers: Go to the "Funds" area of the site and consult the chart of the top and bottom 10 performers over the previous year. If it were I, I'd avoid the Top 10 list and focus on finding good funds that have temporarily found their way to the Bottom 10 list. Remember, it's not uncommon for the high-flying funds of one year to flame out the next year. It's also worth noting that some funds turn up regularly among the bottom-dwellers and should not be given a moment's serious consideration.

- Simple Screening: Click where it says "Fund Quickrank" on the homepage and you'll find a simple screening tool that you can use to find funds meeting specific criteria. For instance, you could ask for a list of global equity funds that are fully RRSP-eligible, have a management expense ratio of 2 per cent or less, have no load fees, and have received a Morningstar rating of three stars or more.

- Detailed Screening: The "Fund Selector" feature is a more complex screening mechanism than the "Quickrank." An interesting twist with this tool is that you can troll for funds that have achieved certain performance thresholds over several different timeframes. For example, you could look for Canadian equity funds that have a 25-per-cent one-year return or more, and a 10-year average annual return of 12 per cent or more. You could further specify that you only wanted funds with four- or five-star Morningstar ratings.

- Hot/Cold Sectors: Go to the "Funds" area of the site and look at the list of best- and worst-performing Morningstar Indices, which are benchmark indexes for mutual funds. Each fund sector has a Morningstar index, from Asia Pacific Rim to precious metals. The performance of each fund index is listed according to its one-day, one-week, one-month, and three-month performance.

If you're interested in mutual funds, Morningstar.ca is a Web site that you absolutely have to visit. That's a strong endorsement, but I'll go one further and say this site is one of the most enjoyable to use and cleverly designed in this book. In fact, if someone asked me to list five Web sites that epitomized the benefits of the Internet for investors, there's no doubt that Morningstar.ca would be on it.

MORNINGSTAR.CA AT A GLANCE:

Who's It For?
Anyone who wants help selecting a mutual fund, wants to keep up with fund industry buzz, or wants educational material to learn more about funds.

Top Things to Do on This Site:
1. Check out the mutual funds that have earned five-star ratings.
2. Read the front-page articles on investing and fund industry developments.
3. Wallow around in the vast reservoir of data on funds.

Don't Miss:
The Fund Focus feature—it's a good bet that you'll find these in-depth write-ups to be more detailed and more intelligent than any fund analysis you've seen before.

Toys:
A fund watchlist that shows you how funds you've selected have done over the previous day, week, month, and three-month period.

LINKS

Globefund.com (www.globefund.com): Some of the top fund research tools around, plus access to a vast archive of articles on funds that have appeared in *The Globe and Mail*. As well, Globefund offers a very good port-folio tracker that lets you include both funds and stocks.

FundLibrary.com (www.fundlibrary.com): Fund research tools can be found here as well, but the real attractions are the columns and articles written by in-house and outside experts. The Fund Library also aggregates the fund ratings of other fund analysts, including Morningstar.

FundScope (www.fundscope.com): This independent fund analysis service charges a subscription fee, but it also allows visitors to use certain services, such as its portfolio risk calculator.

Morningstar.com

> **What's the Deal?:**
> This U.S. mutual fund specialist provides some of the best independent stock research around, plus some great portfolio analysis tools.
>
> **Usefulness Rating:** ✓✓✓✓✓
>
> **Canadian Content Rating:** ✓
>
> **Cost:** Lots of free material, but premium stock research is reserved for paying subscribers.

Morningstar is one of the foremost names in mutual fund analysis, but that's not why this Web site is included in this book. Fact is, you can safely ignore 99.9 per cent of the fund-related articles on this site because they focus on U.S. funds (see the preceding Morningstar.ca profile for Canadian fund information). What you're left with is Morningstar's stock coverage, which is just fine because we're talking about an excellent product here. It's readable, opinionated, and, most appealingly, written for average investors and not hard-driving market fanatics.

You have to be a paying subscriber to read the research reports Morningstar offers on some 1,000 companies, but there's plenty of material available for free. Each day, Morningstar analysts write about the stocks in the news, and they often produce featurey stories as well. For example, I found an article entitled "Ten Stocks To Avoid," as well as a series of articles in which Morningstar analysts picked their favourite stocks in a variety of categories. One article looked at favourite blue chips, others at favourite financially healthy stocks, high-profitability stocks, semiconductor stocks, and so on. The write-up on each of the stocks mentioned wasn't long at all— just a short, pithy blurb, with links to a free Morningstar Quicktake report on the stock, and to a fuller pay-per-view report.

Morningstar on Stocks

The stock coverage on Morningstar is mainly focused on helping investors decide whether a company's shares are worth buying. Here's the site's take on appliance maker Maytag after a new chief executive was named: "We will continue to monitor Maytag's progress closely, but we wouldn't advise purchase of the shares at this time." Now, here's Morningstar on Lehman Bros. after the investment dealer reported a second-quarter net profit gain of 14 per cent: "Indeed on a…forward P/E basis, Lehman trades at a large discount to all of its larger rivals, and the stock's 18.2 per cent decline in the past month looks like a good investing opportunity to us." ■

Morningstar's Quicktake reports are worth using because they incorporate some of Morningstar's own proprietary analysis along with data like financial ratios and annual returns. You can find Quicktake reports on any U.S.-listed stock by using the tickerbox on the homepage. Start off by clicking where it says "Snapshot." You'll get an overview that includes such useful information as:

- Annual returns for the year to date and the three previous years, along with comparative numbers for other stocks in the same sector, and the S&P 500.

- A table of valuations for the stock, including such key ratios as price-earnings, forward price-earnings, price-cashflow, and price-sales.

- A table of key profitability measures, including return on equity and return on assets.
- A table showing one- and three-year growth rates for sales, earnings, earnings per share, and dividends.
- A simple, clear bar chart showing the five-year trend in earnings per share.
- An adjustable graph showing the stock's performance against its sector and the full S&P 500.

All of these data are standard stuff, but they're so cleanly laid out that they just look better here than on many other sites.

Once you've read the snapshot for a stock, look over to the menu on the left side of the page and click where it says "Morningstar Stock Grades." Here, Morningstar analysts assign letter grades to a stock in three categories: Growth, financial health, and profitability. The benefit of the Morningstar stock grades is that they quickly summarize raw numbers in a way that even novice investors can easily understand. For instance, you might not know how to spot a dangerously high debt-to-equity ratio, but you could certainly understand the need to steer clear of a stock with a financial health grade of D.

Morningstar fills out its Quicktake reports with a lot more data, including income statements, balance sheets, insider trading activity, and listings of which mutual funds are buying and selling the stock. Quicktake reports are fine if you know what stock you want, but what if you're looking for ideas about which stocks to investigate? If this applies to you, then go to the Morningstar homepage and scroll down to where it says "Morningstar Tools." Among the tools is a stock selector that lets you screen stocks that meet various financial and performance criteria, or that have achieved Morningstar stock grades of a certain level—say stocks with financial health and profitability grades of B or higher.

I've gone into such detail on Morningstar's stock research because I think you'll find it to be among the best products of its kind on the Web. But there's another feature on the site that is equally impressive—Morningstar's portfolio tracker (to find it, click where it says "Portfolio" at the top of the homepage). The basic technology here is first-rate, but not revolutionary. For example, you can summon up seven different views of your holdings, including ones that provide links to recent mentions of the stock by Morningstar analysts. So what, exactly, is special about the Morningstar tracker? It's a function called a portfolio X-Ray that will do an amazingly detailed analysis of the stocks you own (U.S. stocks and mutual funds only).

First, the portfolio X-Ray will give you a breakdown of the percentage of your holdings in stocks, bonds, and cash. Next, it breaks your holdings down into economic sectors and stock type—examples would be cyclical, slow growth, distressed, aggressive growth, or speculative growth stocks. There's also a "Stock Stats" section that will show you the price-earnings and price-to-book ratios for your entire portfolio, then compare the numbers to those for the S&P 500 stock index. Wondering whether you're on the right track with your portfolio? Then try the portfolio analysis tools—they'll give you re-balancing ideas, and assess how you're doing in terms of saving for life goals like retirement. Note: Subscribers to Morningstar's premium service can do even more in-depth portfolio analysis.

If you like Morningstar's style, then you may want to consider subscribing to its premium-level service. Truth be told, this is one of the few premium financial Web site packages that I've ever even considered signing up for. If you're interested, Morningstar offers a 30-day free trial. Once the trial period is over, you'll pay $11.95 (U.S.) per month, or $99 per year. Included in the premium service is access to 1,000 analyst reports, stock ratings on a five-star scale, a deluxe stock screener, and advanced portfolio management tools. If you're curious to read an analyst report or check out the star ratings, freebies are often made available.

MORNINGSTAR AT A GLANCE

Who's It For?
Investors looking for low-key but thorough independent analysis on U.S. stocks.

Top Things to Do on This Site:

1. Read the coverage of the day's news-making stocks.

2. Read Quicktake reports on stocks of interest to you.

3. Try the stock selector, which is an easy-to-use stock screening tool.

Don't Miss:

The sample Morningstar analyst report made available every day at no charge.

Toys:

A choice of four daily and two weekly newsletters e-mailed directly to you.

LINKS

CBS Marketwatch (cbs.marketwatch.com): A very good general-purpose investing Web site that is definitely worth a look. This site includes lots of stock coverage, but it also keeps abreast of the markets, the economy, and personal finance issues.

SmartMoney.com (www.smartmoney.com): This site gives you lots of market coverage, but its real strength is its high-tech investing tools, including a great portfolio tracker and asset allocation calculator.

Briefing.com (www.briefing.com): Provides opinionated but unbiased market commentary on the day's newsmaking stocks.

TheStreet.com (www.thestreet.com): A savvier, more opinionated version of CBS MarketWatch that will appeal to experienced investors.

The Motley Fool

www.fool.com

What's the Deal?:
The investing Web site with its feet planted most firmly on the ground.

Usefulness Rating: ✓✓✓✓✓

Canadian Content Rating: ✓

Cost: Site access is free, but there are charges for a premium service called Motley Fool Select as well as individual research reports and other merchandise.

Let me make a suggestion that will further your education as an investor. If you're new to investing, or if you've been around a while but you're smart enough to know you don't have all the answers, then make a point of visiting the Motley Fool. Word for word, this site does the best job on the Web of teaching and informing people about stocks and the stock market.

Without taking itself too seriously, the Motley Fool stresses prudent self-reliance in its columns and features. A central tenet in the Fool world is that you are the best person to manage your money. In this spirit, the site doesn't recommend or suggest stocks for you to buy, but rather highlights them for you to study further on your own. "We don't offer our (model) portfolios as models for you to copy," readers are told. "They're funded with our real money so that we can show you how some real investors—relatively ordinary people like yourselves—can build and manage investment portfolios. They're meant to be teaching portfolios. If the market tanks, come see what our portfolio keepers think about it. If a stock surges and swells to represent 50 per cent of one of our portfolios, watch what we do about it."

The Motley Fool began as a newsletter created by brothers Tom and David Gardner in 1993. The online version appeared the next year and has since grown into a small empire including the Web site, a nationally syndicated weekly newspaper feature and radio show, and a series of best-selling books on investing the Motley Fool way.

Where Does the Name *Motley Fool* Come from?

According to the Motley Fool Web site, the name was "chosen from Shakespeare to reflect the spirit of truthful fun that the company brings to the world of personal finance. In Elizabethan drama, only the Fool could speak the truth—and debunk conventional wisdom—without getting his head lopped off." ■

The original Motley Fool project was the Fool Portfolio, started by the Gardner brothers in 1994 with $50,000 (U.S.) of their own money. Now called the Rule Breaker Portfolio, this collection of stocks is worth in the neighborhood of $600,000. Curious to know how they did it? Then click where it says "Investing Strategies" on the homepage and dig in.

Right off the top, you'll find the raison d'être for the Rule Breaker portfolio—to "invest in young companies that are creating or redefining emerging industries"—and the risk level, which is high. You'll also find the latest update on the portfolio, and a link for previous reports. Finally, there's a list of all the stocks, with cost per share, current price, and total gain, as well as a table showing the portfolio's rate of return versus the S&P 500 and Nasdaq. The comparisons are clearly laid out, which means there's none of the ambiguity or fuzziness that makes so many investing Web site model portfolios next to useless.

The other Motley Fool portfolios include the Rule Maker portfolio, which invests in profitable, dominant large-cap companies (medium risk); the Foolish 8, which is made up of small-cap companies with solid fundamentals and bright prospects (high risk); and the DRIP Portfolio, which uses dividend reinvestment plans to invest monthly in leading companies (low risk). In a shining example of the kind of frankness that makes the Motley Fool site so appealing, a commentary I read on the Rule Maker portfolio admitted that things had not been going very well. The portfolio was set up with the goal of outperforming the S&P 500 over five years and, with the fifth anniversary approaching, this seemed out of reach. "It's unlikely the Rule Maker Portfolio will meet its goal of beating the S&P 500 over its first five-year period, but this doesn't mean we're thinking about moving our money to an index fund," the introduction to a report by Tom Gardner said. "We're learning. We're willing to absorb the risk of owning individual stocks. And we believe, with patience and an interest in improving our approach, that we can beat the market going forward." Now there's an investing manifesto for real people.

Analysis You Can Trust

Most serious investing Web sites have a clear policy regarding the investing activities of their writers and analysts. Often, these people are prohibited from owning the stocks they write about and, in some cases, writers are not allowed to invest at all in stocks. The Motley Fool takes a different approach by actually encouraging staff to invest in stocks. The rationale is simple: By being involved with stocks, people are better able to intelligently explain the workings of the markets to readers.

If you see a potential conflict in people writing about stocks they own, you're quite right. That's why the Motley Fool has a disclosure policy that is a model of clarity and directness. At the end of every article, there is a note that informs readers if the writer holds the stock in question. As well, there's a link to an online profile of the writer that includes a list of all his or her stock holdings, and a list of trading restrictions that apply in cases where a writer covers a stock he or she owns. ■

While the Motley Fool portfolios are the core of the Web site, there's lots of other material to read. Click on "News" on the homepage and you'll find several stories by staff on stocks in the news that day, as well as regular features such as "Dueling Fools," where two Motley Fool analysts take a bullish and bearish stance on a stock. As well, there are online discussion forums and a stock research area. This is one Web site where enough new material is cycled through to make it worth visiting on a daily basis.

Lest you think I've gone gaga over the Motley Fool, let me point out its most annoying feature—they are relentless in trying to sell you stuff. While poking around the Fool site one evening, I found pitches for:

- A Motley Fool online seminar on investing basics, cost $24 (U.S.).

- *Motley Fool Select*, a monthly publication that highlights particular stocks. Cost: $10 each, or $49 for a year (an introductory rate).

- *The Motley Fool Money Guide*, a primer on investing and personal finance. Cost: $12.

- "Motley Fool Industry Focus Reports," covering 17 different economic sectors. Cost: $8 apiece.

The sales pitches aren't really bothersome, but they do just faintly undercut the altruistic image the Fools like to cultivate.

THE MOTLEY FOOL AT A GLANCE

Who's It For?
Investors looking for smart market intelligence presented in an amusing and educational way.

Top Things to Do on This Site
1. Study the model portfolios, including the high-performance Rule Breaker portfolio.

2. Read the daily market coverage and how-to investing articles.

3. Use the search function for past mentions of stocks you're interested in.

Don't Miss:

Dueling Fools, a feature where two Fool writers take opposing viewpoints on a stock. This is a great way to get a full view of a stock.

Toys:

A selection of six daily and weekly e-mail newsletters that deliver market updates and digests of Motley Fool stories.

LINKS

CBS MarketWatch (cbs.marketwatch.com): A glitzy, well-executed market news site that tries to be all things to all investors and comes reasonably close.

TheStreet.com (www.thestreet.com): A savvier, more opinionated version of CBS MarketWatch that will appeal to experienced investors.

Briefing.com (www.briefing.com): Similar to TheStreet.com in that it provides opinionated but unbiased market commentary. The presentation is a little rougher, and there's less variety in the stories available.

MSN Money

moneycentral.msn.com and money.msn.ca

What's the Deal?:
MSN Money and its Canadian counterpart are super slick investing and personal finance sites for beginners and veterans alike.

Usefulness Rating: ✓✓✓✓✓ and ✓✓✓

Canadian Content Rating: ✓✓✓ and ✓✓✓✓✓

Cost: Free.

Say what you want about Microsoft Corp., but the company does know how to put out a first-class product. As an example, consider MSN Money. Precious few Web sites of any genre do as effective a job at combining practicality with ease of use and kick-ass design.

Have you ever noticed how the best computer software—yes, some of it by Microsoft—can make complex tasks easy and even a little enjoyable? This is how MSN Money works. It's full of features that bring utter simplicity to complicated personal finance and investing matters. Want to know if a stock you have your eye on is a good bet? Try the StockScouter feature. Think you would like to learn how to research stocks on your own, but are daunted by the jargon and technicalities? Try MSN Money's Research Wizard.

For the full MSN Money experience, try the first URL listed above. The Canadian version of the site was still new when this book was written and, while it showed great potential, it didn't offer the range of features that the main site did. For example, the Canadian site covered three areas—investing, banking, and planning—while the U.S. site comprised six sections, including a "My Money" feature where you can create a customized view of your finances, stock holdings, and news stories of interest. Another useful U.S. feature that wasn't offered on the Canadian site was a "Community" page, which includes message boards, online chats, online seminars, and stock recommendations from fellow MSN Money users.

The highlight of both MSN Money versions is the "Investing" area, but let's focus for now on the U.S. site because it's the richer one in terms of content. There are four key elements here—a high-tech portfolio tracker, a stock research centre, market update information, and commentary by investing columnists. Check out the research tools first, because they're outstanding. To start, go to the MSN Money homepage and click on "Investing" and then on "Stocks." Now, type a stock symbol into the ticker box (the format for Canadian stocks is CA:, as in CA:BNS) and click on the "Go" button. Right away you should notice a few things that distinguish MSN Money from run-of-the-mill financial Web sites. One is that free real-time stock quotes are available, while another is something called a StockScouter Rating. This rating is intended to be an indicator of a stock's ability to outperform the broad stock market. Technically speaking, the StockScouter Rating weighs both fundamental and technical data and then compares the expected six-month return for a stock against expected volatility, or, in other words, risk. A one out of 10 rating would suggest a stock has poor prospects, while a perfect 10 suggests a stock with very strong potential.

MSN Money: A Quick Family History

MSN Money was called MSN MoneyCentral until a retooling in mid-2001 when it was blended with the Web site of CNBC TV, the financial news channel of NBC. The main point behind the renaming of the site seems to be to more closely link the branding of Microsoft's online financial site with its popular personal financial software, Microsoft Money.

The Canadian version of MSN Money is an outgrowth of MSN.ca, Microsoft's Canadian Web site. ■

The StockScouter Rating was developed by MSN Money in conjunction with Camelback Research Alliance, an independent analysis company. Unfortunately, ratings are available only for U.S. stocks and a few Canadian stocks listed on U.S. exchanges—Nortel Networks, for example. In addition to a score out of 10, StockScouter also provides a list of pros and cons on a stock, as well as various charts and graphs. Once you've looked at the StockScouter Rating, you can continue your research by using an extremely versatile charting function that allows all kinds of different views, including many relating to technical indicators such as Bollinger Bands, moving averages, and stochastic oscillators. Analyst consensus recommendations and earnings estimates are also available, as are regulatory filings, insider trading data, and financial results. MSN Money is one of the best sources of data for key financial ratios—to find this information, click on "Financial Results" in the stock research area, and then on "Key Ratios."

A little confused by all of this stock talk? Then by all means take a look at MSN Money's Research Wizard (to find it, click on "Investing" on the homepage and then on "Stocks"). Type in a stock symbol and the Research Wizard will guide you in very simple language through the key questions that need to be asked about a stock being considering as an investment. The questions cover things like a stock's fundamentals, price history, and catalysts that could change investor perceptions of the stock in the future. As the Research Wizard addresses each question, it presents graphs and charts and explains how to interpret them. When financial ratios are used, they're explained in a way that helps you understand what a favourable number is, and how your stock compares to its peers. For combining both hard, useful information with educational value, the Research Wizard is exceptional.

One of my favourite things about MSN Money's Investing area is the analysis and commentary by the site's columnists (check under the "Insight" heading). I would start with Jim Jubak, author of the Jubak's Journal column and senior markets editor for MSN Money. Every Tuesday and Friday, Mr. Jubak takes an informed, opinionated look at subjects ranging from a stock in the news to a particular investing strategy or stocks with promising investment potential. While some online analysts try to dazzle you with investing jargon or bluster, Mr. Jubak has a conversational, jargon-free style that makes for enjoyable reading. I would also suggest you look at the online portfolios maintained by Mr. Jubak: The 50 Best Stocks Today, Jubak's Picks (the best stocks for the next 12 months), and the Future Fantastic 50 portfolio, which is supposed to contain stocks that will grow into blue chips by 2004.

The MSN Money Community

MSN Money's message boards didn't seem to be as active as those of some other sites when I checked, but that doesn't mean you should ignore the "Community" area of the site. For example, it's worth taking a look at the stock recommendations by MSN Money users. If you find a recommendation interesting, click on the user's name to see how his or her previous picks have done. The most-recommended stocks when I checked were Cisco, Microsoft (hmm...), and Lucent. ■

A lot of work has been put into making MSN Money look and work just a little more smoothly than other sites. Take the portfolio tracker, for example. It's so advanced that you have to download Microsoft software (2.5 minutes on a 56.6K modem) for it to work on your computer. A basic portfolio tracker is available without the download, but it's definitely worth going for the deluxe version because the look and functionality really stand out. The total package is good enough to have been named best portfolio manager by *Business Week* in 1999 and by *Yahoo! Internet Life* magazine in 2000.

What's the big deal with the MSN tracker? To start, adding stocks and mutual funds to the portfolio takes a matter of seconds, even Canadian stocks and funds. Funds can be added by using a search mechanism within the portfolio tracker. Be warned, not all Canadian funds are in the database. Once you've got your investments loaded, click the "Columns" button to adjust the configuration of your portfolio to include information on performance, fundamentals like P/E, and dividend yield or asset allocation. If a stock in your portfolio has made the news that day, a "News" link will appear that takes you to a Reuters news story. Want to do some research on a stock in your portfolio? Then click on the "Analysis" button to select charts, analyst info, insider trading data, a company report, regulatory filings, and so on. Bottom line, this is an outstanding way to keep on top of your investments.

The same mix of gloss and utility can be found in the MSN Money stock-screening tools, which you can find by clicking where it says "Stocks" at the top of the homepage. You can do a custom stock search by picking your own criteria, but the real fun here is in using the many pre-set screens. There are six basic searches, including ones called "The Cheapest Stocks of Large Growing Companies" and "Large-Cap Stocks With High Momentum," as well as 11 deluxe screens. My favourite deluxe screen: "Righteous Rockets" which is tuned to pick up profitable, undervalued stocks that are showing fast growth and are beginning to appreciate in price.

The "Investing" area of the Canadian version of MSN Money was sparse in comparison to the U.S. site. For instance, there was little of interest in the "Insight" area, and the portfolio tracker wasn't as sophisticated. On the plus side, the Canadian site's stock-screening tool, while not as refined as the U.S. version, may well be the best product of its type offered for Canadian markets at no cost. Also, you can look up stocks on the Canadian site without having to type CA: in front, and you can find a full range of financial data for Canadian stocks, including key ratios. The Research Wizard feature is also available for Canadian stocks.

The U.S. version of MSN also offers a lot more personal finance content than the Canadian site, but almost all of it will be of interest only to Americans. The Canadian site offered bare-bones coverage of banking and financial planning. No question, there's a lot of potential to fill out these areas of the Web site.

Like any self-respecting financial Web site, both versions of MSN Money also keep you plugged into the markets through the day. If you're interested in what's happening on the major U.S. markets, though, stick to the main MSN Money site. There's market coverage from Reuters, Briefing.com, and CNBC TV, the last of which includes both news items and stock picks by guests of the financial TV operation. A great way to keep up with the hot stocks of the day on U.S. markets is to use the "Top 10 Lists" found in the "Markets" area of the MSN Money Investing homepage. This feature will show you the Top 10 most active stocks, leading percentage gainers and losers, and the Top 10 earnings surprises and insider trading transactions of the previous 30 days. Yes, MSN Money even does mundane things like market updates with flair.

MSN MONEY AT A GLANCE

Who's It For?
Investors of all levels of experience who want help choosing stocks and researching them.

Top Things to Do on This Site
1. Research stocks using the StockScouter Rating and other excellent tools.
2. Set up an online portfolio on what must rank as one of the Web's best trackers.
3. Try out the Research Wizard, a wonderful tool for investors who want to understand stock analysis better.

Don't Miss:
The well-executed portfolio tracker available on both the U.S. and Canadian versions of MSN Money.

Toys:

1. The "My Money" area of MSN Money is a customizable homepage for your portfolio, as well as market news and other types of information selected by you.

2. E-mail investing newsletters.

3. E-mail alerts that tip you off when a stock price has made a big move.

LINKS

Globeinvestor.com (www.globeinvestor.com): Canada's answer to MSN Money Investor can't compete in presentation, but it counters with top news coverage, investing stories from *The Globe and Mail* and a solid database of research on Canadian and U.S. stocks.

CBS MarketWatch (cbs.marketwatch.com): A very good general purpose investing Web site that is definitely worth a look.

Morningstar.com (www.morningstar.com): This site focuses on stocks and mutual funds and doesn't make any attempt to cover the markets per se. The stock analysis will really appeal to middle-of-the-road investors (as opposed to heavy-trading aggressive types).

SmartMoney.com (www.smartmoney.com): A nice mix of investing articles and superb investment tools that includes an asset allocation guide and portfolio tracker.

Multex Investor

What's the Deal?:
Multex is the Web's prime source of equity research reports from brokers and independent sources.

Usefulness Rating: ✓✓✓

Canadian Content Rating: ✓✓✓✓✓

Cost: Free reports available for download, but most will come at a price.

The simplest way to describe Multex Investor is to say it's a very well-stocked online department store that specializes in equity research. Use Multex to search for reports on a particular stock and you might well come up with dozens and dozens of offerings from big and small brokerage houses, as well as independent research sources.

A small minority of the reports are free on Multex. Provided you have an Adobe Acrobat Reader on your computer, you can just click on the title of the report and download it. The majority of reports cost anywhere from $5 to $50 (U.S.)—if you want to download any of them, the price will be billed to a credit card.

Six days a week, Multex highlights a new batch of reports from brokerages of all types. Check the homepage for a list of the day's highlighted reports, including at least a few that are offered for free for a limited period of time, usually a few days. Once you've read through the headlines listing what's available, try using the ticker-box on the homepage to locate research on a stock of interest to you. Let's say it's Pfizer, the big multinational drug company that gave the world the gift of Viagra.

I found three different groupings for reports for Pfizer, the first coming under the heading "Free and Sponsored Reports." Free reports sound good, but they're sometimes not particularly illuminating. For Pfizer, I found a free company capsule from Hoover's Online (Hoover's is an online corporate data firm) that offered little more than basic background on the company and was only borderline useful. Sponsored reports are offered by brokerage houses as part of special offers where you sign up for a free research trial. Merrill Lynch, Deutsche Banc Alex Brown, and Salomon Smith Barney were the firms offering Pfizer reports. To get them, you have to jump to the Web sites for these brokerage houses and sign up for the research trial. This is often worth doing, by the way, because you can sometimes have free run of a firm's library of research reports for a limited period.

The next batch of reports on Pfizer were those available from brokerages. A headline was supplied for each report, along with the number of pages and a price. Be sure to scan the headlines carefully, because they will often give you vital information like whether a firm has changed a rating on a stock. In terms of pricing, a short report or a morning note to clients might go as low as $5, while a standard report might cost $25, and an industry overview that highlights several stocks in a sector might cost $100 or more. The third and final category of research on Pfizer was called "Third Party Reports," which means the research originated from independent providers that are outside Wall or Bay Streets. Independent research is prized by many investors because it's sometimes franker than the material produced by brokerage analysts.

Cool Toy Alert

The Multex Investor Toolbar is a free add-on to your Web browser that gives you quick access to your favourite Web sites, be they investing, sports, or general news sites. It takes about a minute to download the toolbar. When you're done, you'll see it as an unobtrusive row of buttons that fits in just below the toolbar at the top of your browser page.

One of the buttons on the Multex toolbar is titled "research"—click on it and a dropdown menu of research sites selected by you will appear. There are other buttons for quotes, analysis, and so on. You pick the buttons you want and then order them the way you choose. ■

Multex will sell you stock research, but it also gives you the means to do your own investigations. While I was looking at the reports available for Pfizer, I noticed a set of links on the left margin of the page, designed to call up all kinds of pertinent data on the company. For example, there was a link to a page of key ratios, news headlines, charts, insider trading data, analyst consensus recommendations and estimates, and so on.

There are a couple of other odds and ends that Multex provides and they're worth examining as long as you realize that the point in offering them is to get you to linger on the site long enough to find a report you absolutely have to buy. For instance, there's a highly sophisticated stock screening tool called NetScreen (to find it, click where it says "Screening Tools" on the homepage). As well, there's a section called "Investing Strategies" in which Multex staff highlight particular stocks and stock-picking ideas. Often, the stock-picking ideas are based on searches run using NetScreen.

If you find yourself checking Multex on a regular basis, maybe you would like to have the site come to you instead. When you sign up as an accountholder—don't worry, you don't have to provide any credit card information if you don't want to—you can choose to receive free e-mails listing the reports highlighted on the site that day. If you see something that interests you, just click on the link provided and you'll jump right to a page where you can download it. Multex also offers a pair of free newsletters that you can receive via e-mail, the *Telecom Analyst* and the *Internet Analyst*. Both offer bits and pieces of research and analysis and are well worth reading if you follow those sectors.

MULTEX AT A GLANCE:

Who's It For?
People interested in research reports on stocks from major brokerage houses and analysis firms.

Top Things to Do on This Site:
1. Search for research reports on stocks you're following.
2. Check the highlighted reports of the day.
3. Try the heavy duty stock screening tool.

Don't Miss:
"Ask the Analyst" and "Ask the Expert," features where individual investors can pose questions to investing pros.

Toys:
1. Daily e-mails listing the top research reports of the day.
2. Two newsletters that are sent by e-mail, one on telecom stocks and the other on Internet stocks.
3. The Multex Investor Toolbar, an add-on to your Web browser that brings you closer to your favourite Web sites.

LINKS

Wright Investors' Service (www.wisi.com): Free downloadable research reports on about 500 Canadian companies, and many more from the United States and globally. Good background information, with no buy/sell recommendations.

Nasdaq

www.nasdaq.com

What's the Deal?:
Nasdaq's Web site is loaded with useful information for investors.

Usefulness Rating: ✓✓✓✓

Canadian Content Rating: ✓✓

Cost: Free.

A stock exchange's Web site is often like a tourist attraction—pretty to look at, modestly informative, and worth visiting only if you have time to kill. Then there's the Nasdaq Stock Market's site. Instead of spending a lot of money on pretty, ego-boosting graphics, the Nasdaq people put all their efforts into creating a first-class tool for researching Nasdaq-listed stocks. It's true that there's not much on this Web site that can't be found on other investing Web sites, but few of these sites are packaged as cleverly.

Nasdaq.com also does a good job of putting a friendly face on a stock market that for many of us is synonymous with the boom-bust cycle of technology stocks, and with savvy stock traders who often seem to be several steps ahead of the little guy. Fact is, Nasdaq.com has some of the clearest, most easily understood features of all the investing Web sites in this book, and it does a great job of helping less-experienced investors understand financial jargon. Heck, this site even has a pretty good personal finance section.

The heart of the Nasdaq site is an unimpressive-looking quote box that allows you to summon up to 10 quotes at a time for stocks listed on Nasdaq, the American Stock Exchange (a sister operation to Nasdaq), the New York Stock Exchange, or the Over the Counter Bulletin Board. If you're in a hurry, you can choose the "FlashQuotes" feature for a quick overview. If you want to do some serious research, choose "InfoQuotes" instead.

Say you wanted to do some research on JDS Uniphase, which is listed on Nasdaq under the symbol JDSU. Let's look at a few types of information you could get using the InfoQuote feature. This exercise will also serve as a tutorial about how to research a stock on an investing Web site. Here we go.

Fundamentals: To start, let's check JDS's fundamentals, which in this case means basic information on the company, like its number of outstanding shares, market capitalization (shares outstanding times market price), earnings per share, price-earnings ratio, and...wait a minute; what exactly is a P/E ratio, anyway? On most financial Web sites, you'll have to scuffle around to try and find a glossary to answer a question like this. On Nasdaq.com, all jargon terms are conveniently linked to a glossary page. P/E, the glossary explains, is "a stock analysis statistic in which the current price of a stock (today's last sale price) is divided by the reported actual (or sometimes projected, which would be forecast) earnings per share of the issuing firm; it is also called the multiple." You'll find similar explanations for terms like ex-dividend date, current yield, and beta, which is a measurement of a stock's volatility.

The Nasdaq Stock Ticker

Here's a toy that will help you keep a close watch on a group of U.S. stocks and stock indexes on a day-to-day basis. To activate this service, just click where it says "Ticker" on the Nasdaq homepage and follow the easy instructions. What you'll end up with is a ticker box (actually a separate browser window) in which the prices of up to 50 stocks are updated every three minutes. News headlines are also displayed.

The 50 stocks you choose can be listed on Nasdaq, the American Stock Exchange, the New York Stock Exchange, and the Over The Counter Bulletin Board. You can also add 10 different stock indexes to your ticker.

Your ticker box can be adjusted in size and moved wherever you want on your screen. As well, the tickerbox will pop up whenever you click on the "Ticker" button on the Nasdaq.com's homepage. To make changes in the stocks on the ticker, just click on the "Configure" link. ▪

News: When I clicked on "News" on the InfoQuote page I jumped right to the company's most recent news release, which happened to be an advisery about its third-quarter results coming on the following week. Off to the side was a list of the most recent JDS-related news releases and news stories that included the usual stuff from Reuters and PR Newswire, but also items from Canadian sources such as The Canadian Press and Canada NewsWire. As well, there were audio reports about JDS by analysts interviewed on the ON24 Web site (one of the essential sites in this book).

Charting: Time for some charting of JDS stock, which you can do from either the InfoQuote or FlashQuote by clicking where it says "Chart These Securities." The default chart looks at the stock over the past three months, but you can easily call up views for six months, 24 months, and so on, up to 96 months. It's also possible to add various U.S. stock indexes to the chart, as well as up to nine other stocks.

Analyst Info: Too often, investing Web sites present analyst consensus estimates and recommendations in a sloppy, graphically obtuse way that makes the information hard to assimilate. Nasdaq.com has among the best graphics around for presenting these data.

Where analyst recommendations are tallied, green is used for "strong buy" and "buy" totals, while yellow is used for "hold," and red is used for "underperform" and "sell." Nasdaq.com's database of analyst information includes a few features that aren't widely available anywhere else, including:

- Consensus Price Targets: For JDS, there was a graphic showing the stock's current price along with the highest and lowest estimate and the consensus estimate.

- Momentum: Compares the number of upward and downward earnings estimates revisions. A stock has momentum if it shows a significant number of upward revisions. JDS had nine revisions when I checked, all of them down. That's bigtime downward momentum.

- Price-Earnings: Compares a stock's P/E to the average for its industry sector, which in JDS's case is electrical systems/devices. JDS's P/E of 28 was significantly higher than the industry average of 21.

- Earnings Growth: Similar to P/E in that it compares a stock's estimated earnings growth to the industry average.

- PEG Ratio: Uses a bar chart format to illustrate this ratio, which represents the P/E ratio divided by the projected earnings growth rate.

Insider and Institutional Holdings: Nasdaq.com does a particularly good job of giving investors solid data on how many insiders and institutions hold a company's stock, and what they've done with that stock in the past while. For JDS, I found that a total of 831 institutional investors held a shade under 54 per cent of the company. More important, I found that 445 of these had been buying JDS shares recently, while 306 were selling. Among company insiders, there were 38 trades over the previous 12 months, all of them sell transactions. Bottom line here, institutional investors were moderately bullish on JDS, but company insiders were decidedly bearish.

Real-Time Filings: Companies sometimes disclose things in their filings to securities regulators that aren't common knowledge among investors. Nasdaq.com's archive contained 199 filings by JDS to the U.S. Securities and Exchange Commission.

Extended Trading: Nasdaq.com is a good place to go to find out what a stock's doing in pre-market trading from 8 a.m. to 9:30 a.m. and after-market trading from 4 p.m. to 6:30 p.m. I checked on after-hours trading for JDS and found all the usual information you would expect in a detailed stock quote, including bid, ask, high, low, volume, and last price.

Guru Analysis: Nasdaq.com gets this feature from a Web site called Validea, which is mentioned in this book. The guru analysis evaluates the appropriateness of a particular stock under nine different investing styles. For example, there's value investing as espoused by Benjamin Graham, momentum investing by William O'Neil, and growth/value investing by James O'Shaughnessey. The only strategy that JDS really matched up with was contrarian investing as practised by U.S. mutual fund manager David Dreman.

Heatmaps

Heatmaps are a graphic tool for helping investors see where the action is on a given trading day. Nasdaq.com's version of the heatmap is a grid containing dozens of stock symbols. The stocks that are rising are coloured in green, while decliners are red. The more intense the colour, the more pronounced the stock's move. Nasdaq.com offers a pair of heatmaps—one for the Nasdaq 100 index, which comprises the largest, most liquid shares on the Nasdaq Stock Market, and another for the exchange-traded funds that are listed on the American Stock Exchange, Nasdaq's sister operation (see below for more information on exchange-traded funds).

These heatmaps are useful for catching the day's hot and cold stocks at a glance, but they're great for more detailed research as well. Pass your cursor over a stock symbol and an intra-day quote and stock chart will pop up. Left click your mouse on a symbol and you get a menu of functions that includes news, fundamentals, Analyst Info, Holdings/Insiders, and other information on the company.

To find Nasdaq.com's heatmaps, look under the "Market Activity" headline on the left side of the homepage. ■

As for the Nasdaq Web site, the designers have made the home-page a sort of bulletin board where you can keep up with what's new on Nasdaq and other markets. Most of the stuff you'll find here is predictable and disposable, especially the news headlines. A lot more useful is the chart showing the expected IPOs of the week ahead and a special section titled "Today's Events." Here, you'll find new SEC filings by Nasdaq companies, listings of coming stock splits and stocks that have reached new 52-week highs and lows, changes in analyst recommendations, and earnings surprises that occurred that day.

Want more toys? Nasdaq.com also offers:

- A portfolio tracker: Just about every investing Web site has one, but this example has to rank as one of the more sophisticated, versatile, and clean-looking examples that you'll find on the Web. It's also easy enough to use in that you can get a portfolio up and running in about a minute.

- A media coverage search engine: Another service borrowed from Validea. This one lets you pull in the stocks mentioned either positively or negatively on a variety of investing media.

- A stock screener: Again, kudos to Nasdaq.com for executing a commonplace feature in a way that is easier to use and more enjoyable to use than most of the competition. There are 25 different search criteria in this screener, each with a box to enter the minimum and maximum value you want. Don't understand one of the search terms? Just click on the term and you'll jump to an explanation in the Nasdaq.com glossary.

- A guru stock screener: This Validea service lets you find stocks that meet the criteria of one or more of nine investing gurus. See Guru Analysis above for more details.

- Financial Calculators: Some of the calculators can be found through the "Investor Tools" area, but the majority are in the "Personal Finance" section. What an eclectic bunch of calculators they've assembled here. One allows you to compare growth stocks versus dividend-paying stocks, while others will tell you things like your return on a stock if you sold now, and how fees affect rates of return.

EXCHANGE-TRADED FUNDS

Some of the best material on Nasdaq.com covers the world of exchange-traded funds, or ETFs, which are one of the hottest new investment products and a rival-in-the-making for mutual funds. ETFs are something like a stock in that they're listed on stock exchanges, and something like an index mutual fund in that they strive to give you the return of a particular benchmark stock index. In simple terms, when you own an ETF you own a tiny piece of all stocks in the index.

There are a couple of reasons why ETFs figure prominently on Nasdaq.com. One is that there's an extremely popular ETF that tracks the Nasdaq 100 index of the largest, most liquid companies listed on the Nasdaq Stock Market. These fund units are known as Cubes because the stock symbol is QQQ. The other reason is that Nasdaq's sister stock market, the American Stock Exchange, is homebase for nearly 100 different ETFs that track everything from the S&P 500 to the Belgian and Brazilian stock markets.

To look at the Nasdaq.com section on ETFs, click on the main menu where it says "Exchange Traded Funds." You'll find an incredible range of resources for researching ETFs here, including a "Compare All ETFs" function that lets you look at the day's trading action in all ETFs listed on U.S. markets. Click on any fund name and you'll find a fact sheet that will tell you things like the top stock holdings and management expense ratio. There are also reams of information on Cubes and another Nasdaq ETF that tracks the market's biotechnology index. There's a boosterish tone to a lot of the ETF material, but I give Nasdaq.com credit for having the integrity to include a Morningstar.com article that listed both the pros and cons of ETFs. NOTE: All of the material on ETFs can also be found on the American Stock Exchange Web site at www.amex.com.

NASDAQ AT A GLANCE

Who's It For?
Anyone interested in researching stocks and exchange-traded funds listed on the Nasdaq, as well as other major U.S. exchanges.

Top Things to Do on This Site:
1. Research stocks using the InfoQuote feature.

2. Check out the excellent collection of investor tools.

3. Acquaint yourself with exchange-traded funds.

Don't Miss:
Nasdaq.com's financial calculators.

Toys:
1. Heatmaps—a new way of graphically highlighting the hot and cold stocks of the day.

2. The Nasdaq stock ticker—allows you to watch up to 50 stocks at a time, with updates every three minutes.

3. A first-rate portfolio tracker.

100hot

www.100hot.com

What's the Deal?:
Listings of the most-visited Web sites, financial sites included.

Usefulness Rating: ✓✓

Canadian Content Rating: ✓

Cost: Free

Think of the 100hot Web site as the Internet's version of the Nielsen ratings that tell us which television shows are most popular. At 100hot, you'll find lists of the week's most visited Web sites in 14 or so categories, ranging from arts and culture, sports and lifestyles, to business.

Click on the "Business" button on the 100hot homepage and you'll find a few sub-categories of interest to investors, including finance, stock quotes, stock charts, and stocktalk. The finance sub-category contains general investing sites, plus the Web sites of banks, brokers, newspapers, stock exchanges, and mutual fund companies.

It's hard to say for sure, but I'd estimate that about half the 100hot list is slush. The real use of this site is in its listings of general investing Web sites that you may not have heard of yet, or just not gotten around to visiting yet. If you're curious, just click on the site's name and a hyperlink will take you there.

The 100hot site will also interest the voyeur in you. You can look at the 100 stocks that investors have most often sought quotes on that week, the most-often-charted stocks, and the most-discussed investing topics. In each case, the information is provided to 100hot by the entirely reputable Silicon Investor Web site (an essential site included in this book).

Predictably, 100hot is stone cold on Canadian content. Last I checked, the only Canadian entry on the list of general finance sites was Royal Bank. A few Canadian companies frequented the hot quote and chart lists, notably Nortel Networks and PMC-Sierra. As with many investing Web sites, there's a decided tech bias on 100hot, with a few blue chips like General Electric thrown into the mix.

100HOT AT A GLANCE

Who's It For?
Discovering investing Web sites you may not have heard of before.

Top Thing to Do on This Site:
Keep current on the financial Web sites that other investors are using.

Don't Miss:
The list of top-rated stocktalk topics—see what companies and issues are top-of-mind with other investors.

Toys:
1. 100hot will e-mail you daily and weekly lists of hot sites.

2. Access to e-mail newsletters from other services, such as Silicon Investor.

LINKS

Investorama (www.investorama.com): Offers a "Best of the Web" direc-tory with more than 16,000 links to sites classified under a variety of invest-ment-related subjects.

Superstar Investor (www.superstarinvestor.com): Includes 20,000 links to top investing Web sites.

ON24

www.on24.com

What's the Deal?:
Audio clips of analysts, CEOs, and investing pundits talking about stocks.

Usefulness Rating: ✓✓

Canadian Content Rating: 0

Cost: Free

Right up near the top of my "If only I'd trusted my gut instincts" list (investing version) is Apple Computer, which I didn't buy at $14 (U.S.). As I write this, it is trading at $24.85 (U.S.) and looking at more upside. How much more would depend to some extent on a quarterly earnings report due out in a few days. Just to torture myself, I decided to use ON24 to see what Wall Street expected from Apple.

ON24 is a Web site that offers online audio clips of analysts, company CEOs, and investing experts talking about stocks, market news, corporate outlooks, and issues of interest to investors. If a well-followed stock makes news, or is about to as in Apple's case, there's a good chance you'll find a clip of an analyst talking about it on ON24. So it was that I found a clip in which a Goldman Sachs analyst's bullish outlook for Apple was outlined. The quick version: Earnings would come in at the high end of expectations, the analyst said, while management would express comfort with the strengthening numbers projected by analysts. Could the outlook have been any shinier for Apple? I doubt it. Rats.

Don't get the idea here that ON24 is some kind of PR machine because it's not. Consider an audio clip I found in which a Wall Street analyst talked about i2 Technologies. The company, a provider of e-commerce software for businesses, had just released first-quarter earnings and, while the results met Wall Street's expectations, there was also an attempt to lower expectations for the second quarter. The analyst was asked by an ON24 moderator whether there was any compelling reason to buy i2 stock at that time. "My sense is no," the analyst replied. "…We don't think the time is now to commit new money to the stock."

Now, this analyst's comments weren't a revelation or a complete repudiation of the common wisdom on the stock. They were just good, solid commentary on a stock that many investors were following. More important, the analyst's view also served as an endorsement of ON24's credibility and usefulness as a resource for investors. If I'm going to tune into a Web site to listen to analysts discuss stocks, there'd better be comments both positive and negative. Without negative views being aired, the site becomes an exercise in PR and a waste of cyberspace.

ON24's Personalcast

Personalcast is an example of smart packaging by an investing Web site. Just pick a few stocks that you want to follow and create a Personalcast portfolio. ON24 will then provide you with audio clips related to those stocks, as well as research tools that include stock charting, analyst recommendations, and company profiles. Each time you launch Personalcast, the most recent 10 stories related to your stocks will automatically play. If you don't want to hear all the stories, you can select just one or more.

Personalcast is free. To get started, click on the "Launch Personalcast" button on the ON24 homepage. ∎

To get a sense of what ON24 has to offer, go to the homepage and either read the headlines or click where it says "Top Stories" at the top of the homepage. Right away, you'll notice a heavy bias toward technology stocks. You may also notice that a significant number of the analysts who participate on the site are from lower-tier investment dealers in the United States. There's lots of other material available on ON24, but it's not particularly well organized. This means you'll have to click your way through the site to tease out the useful bits.

To start, try clicking where it says "Channels" on the homepage. You'll find 14 or so different story categories, including "Biotech," which looks at new scientific developments in the market; "Analysts," where analysts explain recent calls they've made; "CEOs," where corporate chiefs talk about their strategies; and "Technical analysis," where specialists in this area offer their predictions for future stock-price movements. Two other sections of the site that you'll want to browse are "Programs," where you'll find regular features on a variety of subjects, and "Columnists & Contributors," where you'll find clips from a wide variety of figures from other investing Web sites, including TheStreet.com, Briefing.com, and Individual Investor.

Using ON24 couldn't be easier. You just click on the link for the clip you want to hear and a Real Player window automatically opens to download the clip and then play it for you. The clips are typically about one to four minutes in length, although some longer ones can go on for 15 minutes or so. Using the Real Player software, you can stop, pause, rewind, or fast forward the clip at any point. All clips are introduced and moderated by ON24 staff.

The audio format on ON24 is a bit gimmicky, but there are a couple of reasons it's worth exploring. One is that the clips are often tightly focused on the topic at hand and come right to the point. As well, you get to hear analysts, pundits, and CEOs talk in their own voices. Hearing them talk can help you assess their credibility, plus you're able to listen to them without the sort of filtering that reporters do when they prepare their stories. ON24 does edit its clips, of course, but you still get your information straight from the source. It's worth noting, though, that ON24 would be improved by having transcripts of some or all clips.

ON24 AT A GLANCE

Who's It For?
Investors who want to hear, as opposed to read, analysts, CEOs, and pundits talking about developments on the stock markets.

Top Things to Do on This Site:
1. Check out analyst views on stocks in the day's news.
2. Hear CEOs talk about their strategies and the performance of their companies.
3. Hear the commentary by investing columnists and pundits.

Don't Miss:
The "Columnists & Contributors" feature—it offers content from top online investing experts.

Toys:
Personalcast, an online portfolio that combines audio content with traditional online investing tools.

LINKS

Q1234.com (www.q1234.com): An audio archive of quarterly earnings reports, special announcements, and annual meetings of a good cross-section of publicly traded Canadian companies, including Inco, Dorel, Rogers Communications, Aliant, and SR Telecom.

InvestorCanada (www.investorcanada.com): Commentary on stocks and the markets by mutual fund managers. You can either hear it through the site's audio archive, or read transcripts or summaries.

Q1234.com

www.q1234.com

What's the Deal?:
Listen via the Web to quarterly earnings reports, annual meetings, and special announcements from a wide range of Canadian companies.

Usefulness Rating: ✓✓

Canadian Content Rating: ✓✓✓✓

Cost: Free

Have you ever noticed how some companies are perpetually disappointing? Whether it's through misadventure, bad management, or whatever, they somehow manage to underwhelm investors over and over. Moore Corp. was just such a company for the longest time. Moore built a multinational franchise in business forms, then watched things unravel as the Internet changed all the rules for its products. Moore was a $30 stock in the latter half of 1997; three years later it was struggling to crack the $5 mark.

One day, Moore started to creep higher. All right, I thought after noticing this, what gives? Did Moore finally do something right? Then I happened to notice that Moore was one of the companies that uses the Q1234 Web site to allow investors to listen in to quarterly earnings presentations by its executives. Why not tune in and see what Moore has had to say for itself in the past while? Turns out Q1234 had an archive with two full years' worth of earnings announcements for Moore. Using Real Player software (you can download it for free on the Q1234 site), I tuned into the latest earnings presentation. Then I went back to hear a few previous ones. In each case, I was able to get additional background by downloading written news releases that Moore issued on its quarterly numbers.

Q1234 is one of the more sedate investing Web sites you'll find listed in this book—there are no blaring headlines, no hyped columnists, no pyrotechnical tools. In fact, when I first reviewed this Web site and a related one called InvestorCanada (also one of the 50 essential sites in this book) I dubbed them "Bay Street Unplugged," a reference to a trend of the moment in which rock musicians were releasing albums with acoustic versions of their standards. All you get on Q1234.com is a chance to hear company executives speak in their own words about earnings, business outlooks, and special announcements. It's unfiltered by the news media, so you get to form your own impressions.

Besides Moore, the firms to use Q1234 include MDS Inc., Leitch Technology Corp., Gennum Corp., Royal Bank, Gildan Activewear Inc., Inco, Manulife Financial, and Riocan Real Estate Investment Trust. In other words, a nice cross-section of corporate Canada. If you're interested in a specific company, you can search the Q1234 database for archived and upcoming events. The homepage has a list of upcoming presentations as well as ones that have happened just recently. In all, about 500 events were available on the site when I checked. By the way, companies use Q1234 because it's a cost-effective way to get their messages out to investors.

In Moore's case, I got to hear the company's chief executive and chief financial officer discuss the company's most recent quarterly results, as well as plans to further cut costs and boost revenues. Overall, I found the presentation frank, detailed and, above all, useful in providing some explanation about why sentiment toward Moore was warming. No great revelations here, just a little extra insight for the curious investor.

Q1234.COM AT A GLANCE

Who's It For?
Investors who want to tune into quarterly earnings announcements, annual meetings, and other events held by publicly traded Canadian companies.

Top Things to Do on This Site
1. Listen in to events as they happen, or just after.
2. Use the archives to listen to past events.

Toys:
Q124.com will e-mail you its upcoming call schedule each week.

LINKS

BestCalls (www.bestcalls.com): You'll find a schedule of upcoming conference calls for major U.S. companies here. Some calls that have already taken place are archived as audio files on the site, while recordings of other calls are available if you call a toll-free telephone number.

Quicken.ca

www.quicken.ca

There are roughly a dozen online brokers in Canada, and they all do basically the same thing. You say which stocks, mutual funds, or bonds you want to buy or sell and these brokers execute the trade. Given this common function, should you just pick any old online broker, maybe the one associated with your bank? Uh, no. There are differences between brokers that can have a major bearing on how satisfied you are with their service.

You could do the comparison shopping yourself, but it would be a monumental task. Only by signing up for a broker and trading stocks, funds, and so on can you really judge how good the service is. Want an easy alternative? Visit the Quicken.ca Web site and take a look at its annual Online Brokerage Report (you'll find it by clicking on the "Investing" tab at the top of the homepage). Quicken.ca's rating of online brokers isn't the only one of its kind —Canadian Business magazine does one each year, as do the e-commerce specialists at Gomez.com. I also write one for *The Globe and Mail*, and it's archived on the Globeinvestor Web site. Of all these ratings, the Quicken.ca rating is the best of the bunch in the level of detail it offers.

Say you were interested in BMO InvestorLine, the Bank of Mon-treal-owned online broker that came in first in the 2001 rating by Quicken.ca. By clicking on the InvestorLine name, you will find quick answers to 33 different questions about the broker. Can you set up an account online? Yes. Do they offer wireless trading? Yes. Can you place a stop-loss or stop-limit order? No. By the time you read through all the information provided, you'll have a pretty good idea about whether this broker is for you.

Quicken.ca is more of a personal finance Web site than an investing site, which means it mainly covers issues like taxes, banking, credit, insurance, and retirement. Normally, I find per-sonal finance sites too bland and simplistic, but Quicken.ca livens up its presentation by adding opinionated analysis like the Online Brokerage Report, as well as a similar comparison of online banks. There's also a selection of columns by outside experts such as tax specialist Tim Cestnik and investing experts Richard Croft and Larry MacDonald.

Quicken.ca or Quicken.com...Which Is Which?

Quicken.ca is a partnership between Rogers New Media, a division of Rogers Communications, and Intuit Canada Ltd., which is the Canadian arm of the personal finance software company that counts the popular Quicken and QuickTax programs among its products. Quicken.com is a product of Intuit Inc., parent of Intuit Canada.

Both sites are included in this book. Compare them and see what you think. I think Quicken.com rules overall, although Quicken.ca wins on Cana-dian content, of course. ■

The Investing area on Quicken.ca also includes a routine mutual fund screener, as well as charting, quotes, and news for North American-listed stocks. Strangely, the site does a better job of providing information on U.S. as opposed to Canadian stocks. For example, analyst recommendations were only available for U.S. stocks. Also, U.S. companies seemed to be the only ones available when using a tool for comparing the stocks in various economic sectors according to how they're rated by analysts. All the content on Quicken.ca is so assiduously focused on Canada that it was a surprise to find this shortcoming.

Quicken.ca's portfolio tracker is a nice piece of work in that it offers an easy setup process, includes both stocks and mutual funds, and gives you a wide variety of different options for displaying what's going on with your investments. I also like the way you can call up instant links to charts, quotes, news, and other information on your stocks simply by passing your cursor over the stock's name. Unlike some portfolio trackers, Quicken.ca gives you complete privacy by requiring you to key in a username and password in order to view your holdings.

In keeping with its mission to cover the broad field of personal finance, Quicken.ca provides lots of articles and columns on taxes, home buying, insurance, retirement planning, and small business. Generally, this content is cleanly written and easily comprehensible, even for finance rookies. The site also provides some useful online calculators for figuring out things like how much car you can afford, how much you need to save in your RRSP, or how much tuition fees will be in the future for a university education.

QUICKEN.CA AT A GLANCE

Who's It For?
People who want information on personal finance matters, plus lots of commentary and analysis.

Top Things to Do on This Site:
1. Consult the ratings of online brokers and banks.
2. Read up on taxes, retirement planning, and other areas of personal finance.
3. Set up an online portfolio to track stocks and mutual funds.

Don't Miss:
Quicken.ca's coverage of mutual funds—it's ideal for novice investors.

Toys:
Quicken.ca offers a variety of e-mail newsletters, including an end-of-day market wrap-up and specialty newsletters on mutual funds and small business.

LINKS

Sympatico-Lycos Personal Finance (www.sympatico.ca): The best feature here is a big collection of links to other personal finance and investing sites. Check out "Editor's Picks" for the best links.

Canoe Money (www.canoe.ca/Money/home.html): The Canoe Web site's personal finance section has a solid collection of columnists and a great collection of online calculators.

Quicken.com

www.quicken.com/investments

What's the Deal?:
A quirky, pleasantly low-stress site for researching stocks.

Usefulness Rating: ✓✓✓✓

Canadian Content Rating: ✓✓

Cost: Free

Quicken.com is one of those general-purpose financial Web sites that covers retirement, taxes, small business, and...uh, sorry I nodded off there. There's little in this world as boring as a general-purpose financial Web site. Fortunately, Quicken.com breaks out of the mould with an investing area that is unique and well worth visiting. You can go to www.quicken.com and then click on the "Investing" tab at the top of the homepage, or you can save yourself a step and use the direct URL listed above.

My favourite thing about the Quicken.com approach to covering stocks is that it doesn't cater to market junkies or the super-savvy. Rather, the site tries in a relaxed, entertaining way to throw a wide variety of investing ideas your way. The highlight here, no doubt about it, is the One-Click Scorecard, a tool that evaluates stocks according to how well they fit in with four expert investing strategies. There's the Motley Fool Foolish 8 strategy, which identifies fast-growing small-cap companies; the Warren Buffett strategy (as interpreted by Robert Hagstrom, author of a book called *The Warren Buffett Way*); a growth strategy outlined by the National Association of Investors Corp., and a blue-chip value strategy as defined by Geraldine Weiss, co-author of a highly rated investing newsletter called *Investment Quality Trends*. Just type in a stock symbol and the One-Click Scorecard will evaluate how well the stock fits in with each of the four strategies.

I tried Gillette, a perennial laggard of the moment and a stock that Warren Buffett himself had owned for a while. The scorecard told me that while Gillette is of interest to the Buffett strategy, it wasn't a buy just then. Gillette was of no interest to the NAIC growth and Foolish 8 strategies, and of lukewarm interest to the blue-chip value strategy. Another way to use the scorecard is to pick a strategy and look at a list of stocks that mesh well with it. For instance, you can take a look at a list of stocks that Warren Buffett might like, or at least stocks that Mr. Hagstrom thinks Mr. Buffett might like.

If the strategies on the One-Click Scorecard don't interest you, try the Quicken.com stock screener. You can use the pre-set searches, or fine-tune your own search using 33 different variables. Note that there are explanations on how to use each of the 33 variables—definitely a nice touch.

Let Quicken.com Do Your Stock Screening for You

Quicken.com's pre-set stock screens will hunt up stocks that meet the needs of both value and growth investors. The value screens focus on small- and large-cap value stocks, as well as stocks with high dividend yields. The growth screens go for small- and large-cap growth stocks as well as growth momentum stocks, or those that are fastest growing in earnings and sales over the previous one- and three-year periods. ■

Want more help in finding stocks of interest? Then head to Quicken.com's "IdeaCenter." Good name, by the way. When you read about a stock on a Web site, you should definitely consider it an idea for you to investigate further, and not a recommendation that you should act on. The IdeaCenter on Quicken.com offers a number of regular features, including "My Favourite Stock," where mutual fund managers talk about their best bets, and "the Funnel," which is a roundup of stocks that have been mentioned in the investing media lately.

If you want to research your own stocks, Quicken.com offers a typical selection of tools, including analyst consensus recommendations and earnings estimates, as well as insider trading reports, regulatory filings, and so on. A unique and worthwhile addition to this list is the "the Evaluator," which gives you insight on a stock's growth trend, financial health, management performance, market multiples, and intrinsic value (looks at future earnings minus long-term debt). You'll find a link to the Evaluator after calling up a quote for a stock.

QUICKEN.COM AT A GLANCE:

Who's It For?
People looking for stock-picking ideas in a low-key environment where every gyration of the market isn't given blanket coverage.

Top Things to Do on This Site:
1. Try the One-Click Scorecard, which evaluates a stock according to investing strategies from four experts.
2. Scan the IdeaCenter to see what stocks are mentioned.
3. Use the Evaluator, a research tool that will give you insights on stocks that aren't found on most other investing Web sites.

Don't Miss:
The detailed explanation of how to use the Quicken.com stock screener. It'll help you get the most out of screeners on other sites as well.

Toys:
1. Online portfolio tracking, as well as alerts to tip you off when stocks you own or are watching make a move.

LINKS

Globeinvestor.com (www.globeinvestor.com): A top Canadian investing Web site that offers a deep database of stock research, plus investing and business content drawn from *The Globe and Mail* newspaper.

Yahoo Finance (finance.yahoo.com): One of the best all-around investing Web sites out there thanks to its diverse mix of tools and toys.

RiskGrades

www.riskgrades.com

What's the Deal?:
This site will assess the riskiness of an individual stock or a stock portfolio.

Usefulness Rating: ✓✓✓✓✓

Canadian Content Rating: ✓✓✓✓✓

Cost: Free

Y ou want a low-risk Canadian stock? May I suggest Loblaw Cos., the supermarket chain behind the President's Choice collection of grocery products that people really don't need but buy anyway because they're packaged so well. Of all the dozens of Canadian stocks I analysed on RiskGrades, not a single one offered less risk than Loblaw.

RiskGrades is an utterly superb site not only because of how slick and usable it is, but because it delves into a vitally important subject that doesn't get discussed much in the world of online investing. We're talking about risk here, of course. When you read about stocks on most Web sites, you generally see people talking about price targets and earnings estimates—or in other words, the potential to make money. That's fine because we all invest in stocks to make a profit, but what about the down side? Sure, there's general market risk, but what about questions like how volatile a stock is compared to others, or how much value it lost in its absolute worst years or in general market downturns? If you want to minimize the chances of your portfolio blowing up on you in the next bear market, you would do well to have answers to these questions.

RiskGrades is the place to go for these answers. I suggest you use this site every time you're considering buying a stock, not so much to give you an ultimate thumbs-up or thumbs-down, but to provide an idea of how much risk the stock entails and how much money it might conceivably lose, based on past experience. RiskGrades is the work of RiskMetrics Group, which was spun off from U.S. investment dealer J.P. Morgan a few years ago. Today, RiskMetrics helps more than 5,000 banks, hedge funds, asset managers, insurance companies, brokerage houses, and companies manage the risk of their financial holdings.

RiskGrades works by assigning a score to a stock to reflect its price volatility, also called return volatility, against the weighted average volatility of a varied collection of global equity markets during normal market conditions. The scores can range from a low of zero to as high as somewhere around 8,000, and they can change on a daily basis. What I find most impressive about the RiskGrades

What RiskGrades Said about Loblaw

Risk Ranking: 17% (in other words, 83 per cent of Canadian stocks are riskier)
Highest Six-Month RiskGrade: 172
Lowest Six-Month RiskGrade: 92
Average Six-Month RiskGrade: 118
Minimum RiskGrade in Canada: 5
Maximum RiskGrade in Canada: 3775
Average RiskGrade in Canada: 251

Now you understand why they call Loblaw a defensive stock. ■

method is that it allows for an apples-to-apples comparison of the entire gamut of Canadian and U.S. stocks. Put another way, RiskGrades allows you to directly compare the riskiness of Loblaw, with a RiskGrade of 92 when I checked, against Research In Motion, with a RiskGrade of 699, or Biovail, with a RiskGrade of 317.

The best way to get started with RiskGrades is to sign up for a free membership. After you log in, the first thing you'll probably want to do is click on "Get a RiskGrade" and then run a few stocks through the software. You'll notice that in addition to Canadian and U.S. stocks, you can also check equities from France, Germany, Japan, Italy, Hong Kong, and several other countries. If you just want a RiskGrade score and nothing more, type in the ticker symbol and then click where it says "Go." For a much more detailed and useful picture of your stock's risk profile, choose a "RiskChart" instead. What you'll see is a line graph showing how the stock's RiskGrade has changed over the past six months, and information showing how the riskiness of your stock compares to the rest of the market. Note that you can adjust the timeline on the RiskGrade graph, add additional stocks for comparison's sake, and chart a stock's RiskGrade against its share price.

RiskGrades is even more impressive when you apply its analytical powers to a portfolio as opposed to a single stock. If you think you've properly diversified your portfolio to control risk, RiskGrades will provide a scientific second opinion. To set up a portfolio, click on "Portfolio Analysis" on the homepage and then select "Grade Your Portfolio" from the pulldown menu. Once you've got your stocks loaded, a "Riskmeter" graphic will give you a quick indication of the overall risk level of the portfolio. You'll also get an overall risk score, a comparison of the portfolio's volatility to the most relevant stock index, and, finally, an assessment of the extent to which diversification has addressed risk in the portfolio.

Believe it or not, this is just scratching the surface of what RiskGrades can do for you. There are actually five different portfolio views you can choose, including ones that show you how the overall risk score of your portfolio has changed over selected time periods, and how your portfolio's risk score compares to the individual stocks in a relevant stock index. There's also a graph that gives you an idea of whether the stocks you own are providing sufficient returns to compensate you for the risk they present.

RiskGrades Sounds the Alarm

If you want to be kept abreast of any major changes in the risk rating of stocks you own, you can have RiskGrades send you an e-mail alert. Just click on "Portfolio Analysis" on the homepage and then select "Risk Alerts" on the pulldown menu. You can then set upper and lower limits for the risk scores in each stock in your RiskGrades portfolio(s). If the score of any stock hits or exceeds those limits, you'll get notification by e-mail. ■

RiskGrades is a highly sophisticated Web site that takes a while to learn to use effectively. I'd suggest playing around with it to familiarize yourself, but you're sure to do this anyway because the information presented is so compelling.

RISKGRADES AT A GLANCE

Who's It For?
Anyone interested in learning about the risky side of the stocks they own or might buy.

Top Things to Do on This Site:
1. Get a risk score and chart on individual securities.
2. Run your portfolio through the software to get an overall risk profile.

Don't Miss:
The Asset Selector feature, which you'll find under "Asset Selection" on the homepage. This feature will let you search a variety of stock indexes for securities with risk and return characteristics chosen by you.

Toys:
1. Online portfolios that offer a detailed risk analysis.
2. E-mail alerts to tip you off when the risk score of a stock you own changes.

SEDAR

(System for Electronic Document Analysis and Retrieval

www.sedar.com

What's the Deal?:
The definitive database for regulatory filings by publicly traded Canadian companies, as well as mutual funds.

Usefulness Rating: ✓✓✓

Canadian Content Rating: ✓✓✓✓✓

Cost: Free

SEDAR is a research tool that is made to order for investors who like to burrow inside a company or mutual fund before committing their money. This is where you go for information on public companies and mutual funds after you've looked at past performance, analyst recommendations, and so forth. You might call the stuff you'll find on SEDAR deep research.

SEDAR's mission is to collect regulatory filings, news releases, and other communications related to the activities of public companies and mutual funds, and then make them available for free to all online. Among the types of documents you'll find here for public companies are prospectuses, annual reports, early warning reports, proxy circulars, takeover bid circulars, and management discussion and analysis reports. For mutual funds, you'll find financial statements, annual reports, prospectuses, and statements of portfolio transactions.

Once you have found what you want, just click on the document title and download it using your Adobe Acrobat Reader. There's a lot of minutiae on SEDAR that's of little interest to anyone beyond regulators, but mixed in with it are all kinds of interesting nuggets of information. Say you were interested in a particular company and wanted a rundown on everything it has had to say to shareholders in the past six months. Using the "Search Database" function on SEDAR, you would specify the name of the company and the start and end date for your search. You can further refine your search terms by picking a specific type of document. In addition to searching by company, you can also do so by industry group.

Using an Adobe Acrobat Reader on SEDAR

There are a couple of tricks for using an Acrobat Reader that are especially well-suited to the long, unwieldy documents routinely found on SEDAR. For instance, there's a page-count button on the bottom left of the Acrobat Reader screen—click on it and you will be able to zoom ahead to any particular page in the document you want. If you click on the binoculars on the toolbar at the top, you can do a search for pages that mention a specific word or phrase.

SEDAR can be indispensable when you want to get a closer look at documents that are mentioned in media reports, say a takeover bid circular or a management response to a takeover offer. As well as filling in the details behind business stories in the headlines, SEDAR also lets you track developments at less newsworthy public companies. Are you interested in the shares of Magnotta

Winery Corp.? I found 15 documents filed by the company, including financial statements, a management proxy/information circular, and news releases.

SEDAR's mutual fund area is worth using if you really want to pull apart a particular fund to study it. The fund documents on the site don't generally include the promotional puff stuff that companies typically send to prospective investors. But you will find financial statements and annual reports that contain information like stock-by-stock portfolio breakdowns and investment overviews from the fund's managers. There's also information that can help you understand a little-discussed cost of owning mutual funds— brokerage commissions incurred by a fund's managers in their buying and selling of stocks.

The management expense ratio of a mutual fund, the most common measure of how expensive a fund is to own, does not include the brokerage commissions the fund must pay to trade stocks. If a fund does a lot of buying and selling, the fees incurred could cut noticeably into returns for investors. The best way to measure the impact of these fees is by looking at portfolio turnover, or the percentage of a portfolio that is sold and replaced each year. Some fund companies don't include portfolio turnover numbers in their financial statements, but those that do can easily be found through SEDAR. All you do is pick a fund family and then run a document search. Next, click on any documents titled "Annual Financial Statements."

The quick and dirty way to find out about "portfolio turnover" is to do an Acrobat Reader search using this phrase (see above for instructions). Incidentally, the average Canadian equity fund has an annual portfolio turnover of roughly 35 per cent or so. Lots more than that points to a fund manager with a penchant for heavy trading. Nothing wrong with that per se, but remember that these costs cut into investment returns.

The U.S. Version of SEDAR

Regulatory filings by U.S. companies are collected in a system known as EDGAR, for electronic data gathering and retrieval. Note that several good U.S. investing Web sites—Yahoo Finance and MSN Money are examples —include regulatory filings as part of their stock research tools. If you can't find what you want using these tools, or if you want to do a more exhaustive search or find something filed that day, start your search on a site called FreeEDGAR at www.freeedgar.com. For premium services such as alerts to tip you when a company issues a filing, you'll have to pay for a subscription on a site called EDGAR Online at www.edgar-online.com. ■

As this book was being written, a sister Web site to SEDAR was being readied to provide Canadian investors with data about insider stock trades made by directors, officers, and large shareholders of public companies. The new system is to be called the System for Electronic Data on Insiders, or SEDI, and it will do away with the antiquated arrangement of having insider trades generally reported by provincial securities commissions through printed bulletins. SEDI is the next site covered in this book, so read on.

SEDAR AT A GLANCE

Who's It For?
Investors who want to see the dry but often informative documents that public companies and mutual funds file to provincial securities regulators.

Top Things to Do on This Site
1. Do an exhaustive document search on companies whose stocks you're following.
2. Drill down into the holdings and trading activities of mutual funds.

Don't Miss:
SEDAR's company profiles. They're not particularly detailed, but they will give you such useful information as an address, phone and fax numbers, and a corporate contact name.

SEDI
(System for Electronic Disclosure by Insiders)

www.sedi.ca

What's the Deal?:
A database listing stock trades by corporate insiders at Canadian companies.

Usefulness Rating: not rated

Canadian Content Rating: ✓✓✓✓✓

Cost: Free

Let's say you have a beaten-down stock in your sights and you're looking for a signal telling you it is time to buy. Would it sway you if you heard that top executives at the company in question were buying their own stock? It would certainly get my attention. Insiders are people at a company who have access to important non-public financial data. If they're buying, it suggests a degree of confidence in the future of their company and its stocks (the opposite is true, too).

American investors have long had online access to insider trading data. On sites like Yahoo Finance and MSN Money, you can type in a stock symbol and see a list of recent insider trades. Canadian investors? For the most part, they had to rely on ancient technology —printed insider trading bulletins issued by provincial securities regulators. The only upside is that the bulletins weren't published on stone tablets or papyrus.

With the creation of SEDI, Canadians are now firmly planted in the information age when it comes to insider trading. SEDI is an online repository for all kinds of insider trading data. You'll find weekly summaries of all companies reporting insider trades, the details of individual transactions, and a list of people at various companies who are registered with SEDI as insiders. To give all this information context, there's an event history for each company that shows the timing of stock dividends, stock splits, reorganizations, and so on.

As I was writing this book, SEDI was a month away from being launched. I included it sight unseen because I'm confident it will turn out to be an important resource for Canadian investors, just like SEDAR. Incidentally, SEDI and SEDAR are sister operations in that they are both operated by the Canadian Depository for Securities, which handles clearing and settlement for securities transactions in this country. NOTE: The Web address provided above for SEDI had not been finalized at presstime. If it doesn't work, use the Google search engine (www.google.com) to find the actual address.

Under the reporting rules for insider trades, directors, officers, and large shareholders of public companies will have to report their buying and selling to SEDI within 10 days of the actual transaction. This is a big improvement over the old system, where insiders reported trades to provincial securities commissions by fax, and the commissions made the information public weeks after it was received. One thing to be aware of when using SEDI is that it doesn't include data on insider trades made before the system went live in fall 2001. For that information you will have to return to the old printed records.

SEDI AT A GLANCE

Who's it For?
Investors looking for information on the buying and selling of stocks by insiders at publicly traded Canadian companies.

Top Things to Do on This Site:
1. Check the most recently reported insider trades.
2. View a summary of the week's insider trades.

LINKS

SEDAR (www.sedar.com): This site is a repository of filings to securities regulators by publicly traded Canadian companies and mutual funds. Among the documents you'll find on SEDAR are prospectuses, annual reports, early warning reports, and takeover-bid circulars.

Silicon Investor

www.siliconinvestor.com

What's the Deal?:
One of the top sites on the Internet for seeing what other investors have to say about stocks and investing issues.

Usefulness Rating: ✓✓✓

Canadian Content Rating: ✓✓✓✓

Cost: Free

It took me a long time to warm up to online investing discussion groups, or message boards as they're sometimes called. It seemed that every time I'd go looking for new insights or bits of investing intelligence I would end up finding only sludge. The worst of it was just macho chest-beating, much of it written in a slangy techno-nerdspeak that was semi-literate and fully worthless. This is still the case sometimes, but at least I've learned that some message boards are better than others. Silicon Investor is such a site.

In Internet years—they're like dog years, I think—Silicon Investor is a grizzled veteran. As I write this, the site has recently celebrated its fifth birthday and is rapidly approaching its 15-millionth post. There's a reason why this site has lasted while so many others have disappeared. Simply put, its message boards have a higher quality level than most of the competition. The Silicon Investor tagline says "Smart investors gather here." It's true.

See for yourself. Go to the Silicon Investor homepage, click where it says "StockTalk" and pick a subject. As the name suggests, Silicon Investor does have a technology bent. Still, there's enough variety to satisfy most investors. Overall, there are 35 or so different subjects, including financial and mining stocks, REITs (real estate investment trusts), and defence stocks, as well as semiconductors, computers, and biotech. There's also a section for Canadian stocks, by the way. Once you've got your subject, click on it and you'll go to a list of sub-topics.

Silicon Investor's Canadian Stock Message Board

Here's a selection of some of the more popular subjects I found:

Canadian MoMo Puppies: a discussion of Canadian-listed stocks that trade under $5 and are currently enjoying momentum.

Daytrading Canadian Stocks in Real Time: Similar to the above. Participants submit their Canadian momentum favourites, complete with the price they buy and sell at.

WiLan Inc.: Devoted to the Canadian tech company.

Bombardier, Maker of Planes and Trains and Other Things: Self-explanatory.

Naxos Resources: A company with a gold property in California; listed on the Nasdaq bulletin board.

Geac, a New Era?: Whither this disappointing software company?

Dimethaid Research: Prospects for this drug company are discussed here. ■

Silicon Investor has a simple-to-use format for each of the sub-topics contained within its subjects. There's the original posting that started that particular discussion, then a sequential list of responses that starts with the most recent one. There's also a preview line to give you a quick overview of each message, as well as a mention of the author's name, and the date of posting. For some subjects—the above-mentioned Daytrading Canadian stocks discussion for example—there are specific do's and don'ts to follow. If you want to post a message to any of the online discussions, there's a button to click on for that purpose.

Where the discussion revolves around a specific stock, Silicon Investor provides a detailed quote and a collection of links that enable you to do some fairly thorough research. For example, you can call up consensus analyst recommendations and earnings-per-share estimates from Zacks, detailed financials supplied by Multex Investor's Market Guide division, and a breakdown of institutional ownership of the stock by Thomson Financial.

One way to use Silicon Investor is to go the "Stock Talk" area and browse for interesting subjects. You can also click on "Hot Subjects" or on "New Subjects" to see what other investors are up to. In the Hot Subjects area, each topic is given a Hot Score based on the level of posting activity and bookmarking of this topic in the past 24 hours versus the previous seven days. There's also a list of "Cool Posts" on the homepage. You'll probably find that the most useful way to employ Silicon Investor revolves around the search box on the homepage. Just type in a stock symbol or a phrase and you'll be taken right to any relevant postings. For example, you could type in "T.HML" if you wanted postings on Hemosol Inc., a TSE-listed biotech company (note the T. prefix for Canadian stocks), or "TD Waterhouse" if you were curious to see what other investors thought about this online broker.

Free Real-Time Quotes

A solid bonus on the Silicon Investor site is access to free real-time stock quotes. The actual provider of the quotes is a Web site called FreeReal-Time.com, which is available to investors directly. Silicon Investor also offers a streaming real-time portfolio, but this is a pay service. ■

If you're a frequent visitor to Silicon Investor, you'll probably want to make use of "PeopleMarks" or "SubjectMarks." The method for using these features is explained in the FAQ section of the site, but basically they allow you to bookmark subjects that interest you, or the postings of individual investors you want to follow.

Silicon Investor has evolved from simply providing online message boards to become an all-in-one investing Web site. Accordingly, you'll find top news stories of the day, stock research tools, and a selection of articles culled from other Web sites like TheStreet.com. These features are a nice add-on, but the real action on Silicon Investor is in the give and take among investors like yourself.

SILICON INVESTOR AT A GLANCE:

Who's It For?
People who want to participate in online discussions about stocks and investing issues, or read the comments of others.

Top Things to Do on This Site:
1. See what others are saying about stocks you're researching.

2. Find investing ideas.

3. Learn more about investing strategies and ideas.

Don't Miss:
The "Coffee Shop" message board, where investors shoot the breeze on a variety of topics that often have nothing to do with investing.

Toys:
1. A customized Silicon Investor homepage.

2. E-mailed newsletters—there's a daily market summary newsletter and a twice-monthly newsletter on investing.

3. Online watchlists or portfolios.

LINKS

Raging Bull (www.ragingbull.com): An online discussion forum similar to Silicon Investor, but with slightly fewer toys and gimmicks.

Yahoo Finance (finance.yahoo.com): Popular message boards are part of the wide selection of investing tools on this site.

TheLion.com (www.thelion.com): A Web search engine that finds references to a subject or stock on up to seven different online discussion forums, including Silicon Investor, Raging Bull, and Yahoo Finance.

StockHouse (www.stockhouse.ca): The StockHouse Bullboards are a top forum for investors who want to talk about Canadian stocks.

Site-By-Site

www.site-by-site.com

| **What's the Deal?:** |
| Global stock and stock market research. |

Usefulness Rating: ✓

Canadian Content Rating: ✓

Cost: Free

The world of financial Web sites is much like the rest of the universe in that the sun often seems to rise and set on the United States. The Canadian market gets scant attention, Far Eastern and European markets somewhat more. There's no question that the U.S. markets dominate global stock trading, but this doesn't mean there aren't interesting stories happening all over the world. The question is, how would you go about finding them? One way would be to visit Site-By-Site. With Site-By-Site, you have access to an exclusive collection of financial Web sites from around the world. Looking on your own, it could take you weeks to find these resources.

Click on a region of the world on the Site-By-Site homepage and you'll jump to a listing of all the major countries in the area, along with links to their central banks, their national stock markets, and to sources of information about their local stock market scene. For more developed countries, you'll also get links to recent analysis of their economic situation, and to information on American Depositary Receipts (more on these in a moment) issued by local companies. If you want a broader take on the entire region, Site-By-Site lists a variety of links to news and media Web sites from the area.

I happened to find a large number of links about India while visiting the Asia/Pacific area of Site-By-Site (other regions are the Americas and Europe). The was a link to the Reserve Bank of India's Web site, to the National Stock Exchange of India site, and to a series of economic reports on India by economists at the U.S. investment dealer Morgan Stanley Dean Witter. This stuff was all table-setting for a whole other page of about 60 links headlined "The Indian Stock Market." If you wanted to research Indian stocks—India has some dynamic companies, particularly in software—then this page of links is gold.

Travelling the World with Site-By-Site

Here's a list of countries in this Web site's database:

The Americas: Canada, the United States, Argentina, Brazil, Bolivia, Mexico, Chile, Colombia, Ecuador, Venezuela, Peru.
Asia/Pacific: India, Australia, China, Hong Kong, Indonesia, Japan, Malaysia, New Zealand, Singapore, South Korea, Taiwan, Bangladesh, Sri Lanka, Iran, Mongolia, Macau, the Philippines, Papua New Guinea.
Europe: France, Germany, the United Kingdom, Italy, the Netherlands, Russia, Spain, Sweden, Switzerland, Austria, Belgium, Bulgaria, Croatia, Cyprus, the Czech Republic, Denmark, Estonia, Finland, Greece, Iceland, Ireland, Hungary, Israel, Lithuania, Latvia, Luxembourg, Malta, Macedonia, Moldova, Norway, Poland, Portugal, Romania, Slovakia, Slovenia, and Turkey. ∎

If all you're interested in doing is finding global stock market Web sites, then just click where it says "Stock Exchanges" on the

Site-By-Site homepage. Again, the world is broken down into regions. Pick one and take a quickie overview of all the major stock exchanges in the area. Out of nothing more than idle curiosity, I checked out the Athens Stock Exchange Web site—it's simple but potentially quite useful if you ever need information on listed companies. And yes, as is usually the case with Site-By-Site, the link takes you to an English version of the Web site.

There are several other groupings of links on Site-By-Site, including some for derivative exchanges, central banks, and global economic commentary. This latter one includes several notable resources, including the Web site of Ed Yardeni, chief investment strategist of Deutsche Banc Alex. Brown in New York (yes, he has his own Web site), as well as the World Bank, the Organization for Economic Cooperation and Development, and the G8 Information Centre, which happens to be located at the University of Toronto. Another set of links covers American Depositary Receipts, or ADRs, which are a kind of security that allows global companies to make their shares available to investors through a listing on one of the major U.S. stock exchanges.

CLOSED-END FUNDS ON SITE-BY-SITE

"Closed-end funds are becoming more and more popular.
Yet information is either difficult to get, limited or costly."
—The Site-By-Site Web site.

Maybe Site-By-Site knows something I don't about closed-end funds. Aside from a reader of *The Globe and Mail* in British Columbia who's always urging me to write about a particular closed-end fund called United Corporations Ltd., I don't think I've ever heard anyone voice enthusiasm over this type of investment. Where I will agree with Site-By-Site is on the point about closed-end funds being impossibly tough to research.

Site-By-Site solved the problem by linking up with a Web site called Closed-End Fund Center (www.cefa.com). Just click where it says "Closed-End Funds" on the Site-By-Site homepage and you'll find a menu of fund categories. Choose one and you'll find a list of all major funds in the category, each of them linked to an information page on Closed-End Fund Center. This would be a good point to explain what closed-end funds are, and why they might be of interest. Think of closed-end funds as a regular mutual fund (also called an open-ended fund) that is bought and sold like a stock on a stock exchange. Like regular mutual funds, closed-end funds employ managers whose job it it is to choose stocks and bonds. The big attraction of closed-end funds is that they often specialize in global market niches that regular mutual funds in Canada haven't exploited yet. Here are three examples culled from by Site-By-Site's listings:

The Brazil Fund (BZF-NYSE)—Holds the shares of Brazilian companies, as well as bonds issued by the Brazilian government.

Morgan Stanley Africa Fund (AFF-NYSE)—Focuses on Morocco and South Africa, but also may include developing African economies as opportunities arise.

Templeton Emerging Markets Income Fund (TEI-NYSE)—Invests in bonds issued by corporations and governments in emerging markets.

Beware the Discount

One thing to be wary of with closed-end funds is that their units sometimes sell at a discount to their net asset value per share. Poor investor sentiment about the sector a fund invests in may contribute to a discount. There's also a perception that closed-end fund managers aren't as aggressive as open-end managers, who work in a more commercial environment and are under greater pressure to attract unitholders. Fans of closed-end funds say discounts can provide attractive buying opportunities, and they can as long as the discount narrows or even disappears at some point. With some funds, though, the discount is ever-present. Note also that hot closed-end funds may trade at a premium. Be careful in these cases—the premium can quickly disappear if the fund hits a bad patch. ∎

I don't usually like to comment on a Web site's looks because of the possibility that a redesign will improve the situation. With

Site-By-Site, I'm fairly confident this won't happen because I have seen it through a few different designs over the years and all have been, shall we say, uninspired. It's not a big problem because the site is easy to navigate. Still, you might be inclined to think Site-By-Site isn't a serious enterprise because of its appearance. That would be wrong.

SITE-BY-SITE AT A GLANCE

Who's It For?
Anyone who wants information on the stock market scene in countries around the world.

Top Things to Do on This Site:
1. Research global stocks and stock markets.
2. Look for economic commentary and statistics on all major global economies and regions.
3. Research closed-end funds that focus on regions and individual countries around the world.

Don't Miss:
The page of links on the U.S. market. It's a ragged but varied collection that will almost certainly show you financial Web sites you haven't already heard about.

LINKS

ADR.com (www.adr.com): An amazing array of resources for researching the shares of global companies that have American Depositary Receipts, or ADRs, trading on U.S. markets.

Worldlyinvestor.com (www.worldlyinvestor.com): This independent stock research site mainly covers U.S. stocks, but it also offers weekly columns on emerging market stocks, Asian stocks, and European stocks.

Financial Times (www.ft.com): The venerable *Financial Times* newspaper's Web site provides global coverage of economics and market developments. There is also extensive emerging market coverage, plus detailed coverage of the U.S., British, Asian, and European stock markets.

SmartMoney.com

www.smartmoney.com

What's the Deal?:
An superb collection of investing articles and tools.

Usefulness Rating: ✓✓✓✓

Canadian Content Rating: ✓✓

Cost: Free

So, what's your asset allocation? Are you indifferent to risk and therefore loaded to the gunwales with stocks, or are you a middle-of-the road type with money spread among stocks, bonds, and cash? Asset allocation may sound like dreary investing jargon, but it's actually one of the most important aspects of portfolio planning. By some estimates, it accounts for about 80 per cent of your returns, making it vastly more important than the actual choice of stocks, mutual funds, and bonds that you buy.

One of the key tasks an investment adviser will take on for you is to create an asset allocation model for your portfolio. But what if you're a do-it-yourself investor and want to create your own model? Investing Web sites love to help you pick stocks, but few show any interest in the more important question of how much you should invest in stocks. A notable exception here is SmartMoney.com, which has some of the niftiest portfolio management tools on the Web.

SmartMoney.com is a Web offshoot of *SmartMoney* magazine, which is billed as *The Wall Street Journal's* personal finance magazine. *SmartMoney* is a joint venture between Hearst Communications and Dow Jones, which means there's big money behind the magazine and Web site. It shows. Curious to see what I mean? Then click where it says "Tools" on the SmartMoney.com homepage, and again on "Asset Allocator" (listed under the heading "Your Investments"). What you'll find is an interactive asset allocation worksheet that asks you to specify how much of your assets are in cash, bonds, small-cap stocks, large-cap stocks, and international stocks. You'll also be asked for your tax bracket (unfortunately, these are U.S. brackets, which are lower than Canadian ones). Your next step is to answer questions like how many years until you want to retire, how much is in your retirement account, and so on.

SmartMoney University

Most of the articles you'll find on SmartMoney.com are quite accessible, even for investors with only modest experience and knowledge. If you've a novice, you'll still find lots of useful content, though. Just scroll down the homepage to where it says "SmartMoney University." There, you'll find a good selection of primer-like articles on investing and personal finance topics. ■

When you're done, you will find that SmartMoney.com has created a colour-coded pie chart showing your current asset allocation. Are you on the right track with your diversification efforts? To find out, click where it says "ideal allocation" and watch the pie chart reconfigure itself to show you where you should be based on your personal situation. The appeal of this tool is that it shows you in very clear, graphic terms how different factors affect your ideal asset allocation. For example, as you move your risk tolerance down, the wedge of the pie devoted to bonds grows while the stock wedge shrinks.

To use SmartMoney's portfolio tracker is to laugh at the retrograde crap most other financial Web sites give you. To start, there's the traditional chart showing how much you paid for each stock, what price each stock is trading at, how much it's up or down on the day, the current value of your holdings, and so on. From there, things start to get interesting. Click on the "Map" icon and Smart-Money.com will create a graphic for you in which each of your holdings is represented by a square that reflects the stock's proportional size in your portfolio. As well, each square is colour-coded to show you whether it rose or fell sharply, or was modestly up or down. The overall impact is striking. At a glance, you can tell how each of your stocks has done on the day, and how prominently each stock figures in your portfolio.

Now click on the "Allocation" button. Instantly, SmartMoney will produce a large pie chart to show you how much of your holdings are in the various asset categories. Click on the "Analysis" button and you'll find a unique chart that will show you how your stocks compare to each other in a variety of performance categories, including one-, three-, or five-year total return, market value, revenues, earnings growth, forward price-earnings ratio, percentage off 52-week high or low, and more. Spend just 10 minutes with this tool and you can't help but have a better understanding of the stocks in your portfolio.

Canadian Stocks on SmartMoney

The good news is that you can plug Canadian stocks into the portfolio tracker—all you have to do is type @TOR after the ticker, as in TOC@TOR. Unfortunately, you'll find scant data for Canadian-listed stocks. This means you won't get much use out of the portfolio tracker's analysis function, although mapping will work in most cases. ■

Like the portfolio mapping function? If you do, then check out SmartMoney's "Map of the Market" (click on "Maps" at the top of the homepage). Using the same arrangement of coloured squares, the market map gives you a definitive picture of the how the various sectors in the markets are doing that day, and which stocks dominate those sectors. You can tweak the mapping software to show things like headlines for stocks on the move, or to highlight the top five gainers or losers in each stock sector.

SmartMoney's tools are the best reason to visit this site, but there's almost always a lot to read, as well. Be sure to check for investing articles from the most recent issue of *SmartMoney* magazine. Cover stories in particular are usually available on the site, along with charts that show you updated prices on any stocks that are suggested. It's also worth looking under the "Analysis and Commentary" banner on the homepage for articles of interest.

Naturally, SmartMoney offers full-scale coverage of the day's stock market goings-on. You can start with a market wrap story, or click on individual news stories. Another option is to read the "Daily Briefing," which gives you quick hits on the day's hot stocks, as well as listings of stocks that have been upgraded and downgraded by analysts, corporate earnings reports, and the day's initial public offerings, or IPOs. There's more market coverage under the "Stocks" banner on the homepage.

There's really only one thing wrong with SmartMoney.com, and it's hardly fatal. The site's archive only goes back five days, which isn't long at all. You can get around this by visiting often, which you'll probably want to do anyway.

SMARTMONEY.COM AT A GLANCE

Who's It For?
People looking for a true all-things-to-all-investors site.

Top Things to Do on This Site:
1. Set up the excellent portfolio tracker.
2. Try the asset allocation tool.

3. Read through the many useful articles on investing and personal finance.

Don't Miss:
"Map of the Market," a powerful graphic tool for showing you what's happening on the stock market.

Toys:
The site's loaded with them. Have fun.

LINKS

CBS MarketWatch (cbs.marketwatch.com): Another very good general purpose investing Web site that is definitely worth a look. This site plays up its analysts and commentators more than SmartMoney.com does.

Morningstar.com (www.morningstar.com): This site focuses on stocks and mutual funds and doesn't make any attempt to cover the markets per se. The stock analysis will appeal to middle-of-the-road investors as opposed to heavy-trading aggressive types.

Stingy Investor

www.stingyinvestor.com

Stingy Investor is the personal playground of a Toronto-based physics Ph.D.-turned-investing-expert named Norman Rothery. There are many such sites on the Web and most of them can be dismissed as vanity projects, or hobbies at best. Mr. Rothery's site qualifies as being more than that.

For one thing, Stingy Investor has enjoyed a longevity that is rare in the online world. The site began in 1995 as Directions: An Investor's Guide to North American Equities, then underwent a modest repackaging into Stingy Investor in 2000. As a financial journalist, I found Directions to be the first good online source of information about discount brokers in Canada. Showing great enterprise, Mr. Rothery compiled pages and pages of data to help investors compare commissions and features at both Canadian and U.S. discount brokers.

Stingy Investor retains the broker listings, and they're a valuable resource if you plan to open an account with an online broker (or discount broker as they're also called). There are many other reasons to be visit this site, though. To start, click where it says "Articles" on the homepage to view articles that Mr. Rothery has written for the site and for *Canadian MoneySaver* magazine. Among the articles I found was a look at how mutual fund management fees eat away at investment returns, an explanation of how to use online stock screens, a dissertation on a stock-picking technique involving something called the Value Ratio, and a discussion of the merits of index funds versus actively managed funds.

Premium Stinginess

Stingy Investor is like a growing number of investing Web sites in that it provides a good free service, while reserving premium content for paying subscribers. An introductory subscription to Stingy Investor's high-grade service costs $99, while a regular subscription costs $199. The flaw here is that the site doesn't give you much of a taste of the deluxe content you'll be paying for. If you like the Stingy Investor and are interested in subscribing, I suggest you send an e-mail to request more information on what you get for the money. ■

As you would expect from the title, Stingy Investor professes to be focused on "the frugal individual investor." Mr. Rothery is not crazy about mutual funds, although Stingy Investor does publish regular fund reports from Dan Hallett, analyst at a discount fund dealer called Sterling Mutuals. Also, Mr. Rothery is not into trends or fads, so don't bother looking for his thoughts on Internet stocks. What you do get are thoughtful little investigations that are meant to get you thinking about a subject, rather than telling you exactly what to do.

A good example of this approach is the "Stocks" section of the site. Mr. Rothery has created several screens you can use to sift through Canadian and U.S. stocks to find ones that meet classic criteria for value investing. In each case, Mr. Rothery explains the theory behind the screen and then lets you run a search using current market data. When you get the results of your screen, there's a full explanation of how to interpret everything. There are slicker, easier-to-use stock screens on the Web, but few of them are as focused as Mr. Rothery's. Moreover, his screens cover the Canadian market, while the best screens on other sites mainly do the U.S. markets.

Dividend reinvestment plans are an obvious area of interest for frugal do-it-yourself investors, so Stingy Investor has created one of the better online databases on this subject. You'll find a list of Canadian companies offering DRIPs (as well as a similar set-up called Share Purchase Programs, or SPPs), complete with links to stock quotes and charts. There were also links to Web pages where you could download documents to sign up for company DRIPs, but none of them worked when I tested them.

Stingy Investor's listings on discount/online brokers are worth reading, even if some of the material is outdated. For instance, I found references to CT Market Partner, a discount broker taken over by TD Waterhouse a while ago, and even to TD Green Line, the name that Waterhouse used in Canada until a few years ago. Mr. Rothery's broker coverage also includes a commission calculator— just specify how many shares you want to buy and at what price, and the calculator will tell you the cost at various different brokers for both phone and online transactions. Be sure as well to look at the broker forums in the "Brokers" section of Stingy Investor. This isn't a very active online discussion site, but I found at least a few up-to-date investor comments on most of the larger brokers. Most participants use the forum to vent frustrations, so don't expect to find much positive word of mouth.

STINGY INVESTOR AT A GLANCE

Who's It For?
Anyone interested in the thoughts and musings of an out-of-the-mainstream investing enthusiast who favours a conservative, do-it-yourself approach.

Top Things to Do on This Site:
1. Browse through the list of investing articles.
2. Check out the broker database, if you're interested in finding an online broker.
3. Try the stock screens tailored to find defensive value stocks.

Don't Miss:
The mutual fund research reports contributed by analyst Dan Hallett of Sterling Mutuals, a discount fund dealer.

Toys:
1. A commission calculator that tells you how much a stock trade will cost at a wide range of online brokers.
2. A selection of daily and weekly reports that can be e-mailed to you at no cost.

StockCharts.com

What's the Deal?:
Mandatory viewing for investors who use technical analysis to pick stocks.

Usefulness Rating: ✓✓✓✓

Canadian Content Rating: ✓✓

Cost: Free basic service; premium service costs $199.95 (U.S.) per year.

P eople who seriously take up investing in stocks are going to realize at some point that they could really benefit from an understanding of technical analysis. When it happens to you, the best thing to do is to lie down and wait for the feeling to pass. If you still want a challenge, try something simple like reading *War and Peace* in the original Russian. Yes, technical analysis is that confounding. What a help it would be to find a resource that would simplify the subject to a point where you could actually put it to work for you.

StockCharts.com is such a site, but I have to warn you not to expect a Technical Analysis for Morons approach. On StockCharts, you'll find a great collection of charting tools that you won't be able to use unless you either have a good working knowledge of technical analysis, or you're willing to learn. Appropriately, the how-to section of StockCharts is called "Chart School."

"Chart School" is, well, like school. "Technical analysis is the examination of past price movements to forecast future price movements," you're told off the top. From there, you'll be introduced to axioms like "what is more important than why," as well as "price discounts everything" and "price movements are not totally random." Once the introductory spiel is done, you'll get into the guts of technical analysis by looking at support levels, momentum, and so on. "Chart School" takes about 20 minutes and is well worthwhile because it gets you in shape to use the excellent charting tools offered on StockCharts. If you need more help, and you may well, there's also a glossary and archive of columns by in-house technical analysts.

To get an overview of the different types of charts available on StockCharts, click on "Tools & Charts" at the top of the homepage. StockCharts calls its top charting tool "Sharp Charts," and you can use them to create charts of any U.S.-listed stock, stock index, or mutual fund. Many key technical indicators are included in these charts, including moving averages and Bollinger Bands. "Sharp Charts" can be customized to the nth degree—in many cases, you can use your own settings or defer to chart parameters used by experts. If you run into trouble, there's a set of instructions to help.

Market Carpets

This amazing graphic tool basically makes a colourful patchwork carpet out of several major stock indexes, including the Toronto Stock Exchange. Each sector of the market gets its own section of the carpet, and each section is broken down into small squares for individual stocks. Pass your cursor over the stock squares and a box pops up to give you a quick bite of data on how the stock is doing in terms of its price, or several different technical indicators.

The presentation is simplified by the fact that the squares of stocks and sectors that are up on the day are in green, down sectors are red, and flat sectors are beige. The beauty of this is that you can immediately zero in on hot or cold areas of the market and find out which stocks are moving. Market carpets can be found under Tools & Charts. ■

StockCharts was created in 1999 by Chip Anderson, a veteran of Microsoft Corp. While there's no apparent connection between Microsoft and StockCharts, the site does have a Microsoft-like slickness to it, and I mean that in an entirely complimentary way. "What's different about our tools is that they allow you to interact directly with the data—dragging, sliding, drawing, zooming it until you see exactly what you are interested in," the site explains. Beyond the already-mentioned "Sharp Charts," there are "PerfCharts," which allow you to compare several different stocks, funds, or indexes (again, U.S.-listed only), as well as "Point & Figure Charts," which filter out less significant price moves from a securities chart. Two other features worth noting are a screening tool called "Technical Scans," and "Voyeur Charts," which allow you to look at charts recently requested by other StockCharts users.

StockCharts offers a laudable free service, which means that only hardcore technical analysis freaks would be interested in the premium package. If you're curious about what the premium package adds, there's a handy page available that compares it to the standard service. The cost of moving to StockCharts Extra is $19.95 (U.S.) per month, or $199.95 per year.

STOCKCHARTS AT A GLANCE

Who's It For?
Charting heaven for the technical analysis crowd.

Top Things to Do on This Site
1. Use the interactive charting options to look up U.S.-listed stocks, stock indexes, and mutual funds.
2. Compare charts of various stocks and stock indexes.
3. Scan entire stock markets for opportunities using "Market Carpets."

Don't Miss:
"Voyeur Charts," which let you take a peek at charts requested by other StockCharts users.

Toys:

1. Create a list of favourite charts.

2. E-mail charts to other investors.

LINKS

Stockscores (www.stockscores.com): This site scans the major stock markets from a technical analysis point of view and provides you with signals that suggest whether the stock is on the rise or decline.

Stockscores

www.stockscores.com

What's the Deal?:
Technical analysis harnessed in a way that can help you find short-term stock-trading opportunities.

Usefulness Rating: ✓✓✓

Canadian Content Rating: ✓✓✓✓✓

Cost: Free

Like the preceding Web site, StockCharts.com, Stockscores is aimed at followers of the inscrutable art of technical analysis. The difference is that StockCharts gives you the tools and lets you run with them, while Stockscores gives you some very useful guidance on where to look for opportunities in the market.

Through each trading day Stockscores takes virtually all North American-traded stocks and assesses their trading patterns. It then assigns a pair of scores for each stock, one called a Signal StockScore and the other a Sentiment StockScore. A Signal StockScore of one to 29 is considered bearish, while 30 to 39 means caution, 40 to 59 means neutral, 60 to 69 means optimistic, and 70 or higher means bullish. Sentiment StockScores are translated along similar lines.

The point of these scores is to give you an indication of whether a stock represents a short-term buying or selling opportunity. Note the word *indication* here. Stockscores isn't designed to flash "Buy" or "Sell" messages in neon lights, but rather to give you a starting point for your own investigation using technical analysis. As the Stockscores site itself notes, "Some [stocks] will be good opportunities, but most will either be opportunities already missed or situations worth monitoring but not yet appropriate."

Your Stockscores Portfolio

The Stockscores portfolio tracker works a bit differently from most in that it doesn't monitor the performance of your stocks so much as it does their Stockscores. Once you've loaded in your stock symbols, you can view the signal and sentiment stock scores for each, as well as a technical chart. Viewing your portfolio is almost like watching a slideshow. Each stock gets its own page, and you can click backwards or forwards through your holdings. ■

How do you tell whether a stock is a promising trading opportunity or a dud? Stockscores can help you there by providing a wide variety of technical indicators based on price and volume. If you're unclear on how all of this stuff works, click where it says "School" at the top of the homepage and study the easy-to-read educational material.

One way to use Stockscores is to call up a report on a stock that you're following (for stocks listed on the Toronto Stock Exchange, always type T. in front of the symbol, as in T.BCE), while another is to use the "Sector Watch" function to look for the Stockscores of equities in the major sectors of the big U.S. and Canadian markets. There's a Stockscore for each sector overall, as well as for the stocks within it. If you're curious about the ratings of the day's big movers on the markets, check the bottom of the Stockscores homepage. There, you'll find a list of the most active stocks on major North American exchanges, complete with their scores and ratings of bullish, optimistic, neutral, and so on. Still another option is to use the

"Market Scan" function, which is a screener that will help you find stocks using various technical indicators. There are also pre-set screens to search for stocks—one is a bottom-fishing screen, while another is supposed to find stocks that may be headed lower following a big surge.

The best thing about Stockscores is the way it provides a window into the realm of technical analysis for outsiders. You may never master technical analysis, but you can always use Stockscores to get a reading on whether or not stocks you're interested in are technically strong. Now, that's a unique and useful service.

STOCKSCORES AT A GLANCE

Who's It For?
People interested in using technical indicators to find short-term stock-trading opportunities.

Top Things to Do on This Site
1. Check the Stockscores of individual stocks.
2. Create a portfolio of stocks and monitor their Stockscores on an ongoing basis.
3. Use the screening strategies to find investing opportunities, or set up your own screen using technical indicators.

Don't Miss:
The daily tutorial, found on the homepage—it offers a quick lesson on a strategy using technical analysis, and it highlights a stock each day that fits in with the strategy.

Toys:
Stockscores offers a weekly e-mail newsletter.

LINKS

StockCharts (www.stockcharts.com): Killer charting tools for people who are already adept at technical analysis, or are willing to learn using the site's ample educational resources.

StockHouse

What's the Deal?:
One of Canada's top online discussion forums for investors, plus an archive of media articles on the markets.

Usefulness Rating: ✓✓

Canadian Content Rating: ✓✓✓✓

Cost: Free basic services, plus a premium package for paying subscribers that starts at $24.95 per month.

Stock House was an iffy inclusion in this book because of questions about its prospects for long-term survival. At press time, StockHouse was like many Web sites of all types in that it was labouring to make it through a weak market for online advertising and a total lack of interest among investors in putting money into dotcom ventures. I liked StockHouse's chances, and the services it offered, so I took a chance and made it one of the 50 essential sites.

Off the top, I have to note that StockHouse ain't what it used to be. A cost-cutting drive in mid-2001 chopped away almost all of the excellent original reporting, analysis, and columns that made the site indispensable for Canadian investors looking for help in picking their way through the stock scene. So why is the site here in this book? Because it still offers some very useful investing tools, notably its BullBoards. The StockHouse BullBoards are possibly the best online discussion forum you'll find for Canadian stocks. All of the big U.S. forums—Silicon Investor, Yahoo Finance, and so on— have active discussions on Canadian stocks, but the StockHouse BullBoards often have wider participation. That means more post-ings, more views expressed and, thus, more utility for the investor who wants to hear all the gossip about a particular stock.

The main BullBoards page on the StockHouse site lists all the latest postings by stock symbol. Underneath, there's a list of the most popular postings, as measured by the number of times they have been viewed. If you're curious about the stocks most often discussed, there's a listing of the Top 10 boards. You'll quickly notice when checking these lists that speculative plays and small-cap stocks are a favourite on StockHouse. Stocks that came up repeatedly when I checked the site included Itemus Inc. and Nexus Group International Inc., a pair of Internet companies, as well as 360Networks Inc., the struggling fibre optics company.

Larger, more established stocks are actively discussed on the Bull-Boards as well. Not surprisingly, there's a well-used board on Nortel Networks. Resource stocks like Inco and Noranda are reasonably busy as well, as are boards on the big banks. If you want to see what the buzz is on a particular stock, there's a function that lets you search the BullBoards database by stock symbol, by company name, or by the username of a particular BullBoard participant.

Back in its heyday, StockHouse employed reporters and columnists who pumped out a lot of topnotch stuff every day on Canadian stocks. Now, most of the content on the site comes from outside sources, including newspapers like the *National Post*, magazines like *Canadian Business* and wire services like The Canadian Press and Bloomberg. I liked the old way better, but it's a lot cheaper to use other people's content than to pro-duce your own. Anyway, StockHouse's premium service offers some compensation for the lack of originality of the site's invest-ing articles. It's called MediaScan and it's a great tool for investors who want to find mentions of a particular company or stock in one or more of some 600 different media sources. Among these sources: Dow Jones, Bloomberg News, the *Financial Times*, ABC News, *Fortune* magazine, the Motley Fool Web site, Yahoo, and dozens of newspapers from around the world.

Maybe you're curious about what's been said about Royal Bank in the U.S. and Canadian investing media over the previous few months. With MediaScan, all you have to do is type in the bank's stock symbol, RY, then limit the search to either U.S. or Canadian media sources and choose a timeframe. I tried this search over a one-month period and came up with all of one U.S. reference, which was in a story that appeared on TheStreet.com. For Canadian references, I got more than 100 hits from sources ranging from Bloomberg News, Dow Jones, and The Canadian Press to several major daily newspapers, including *The Globe and Mail*.

STOCKHOUSE AT A GLANCE

Who's It For?
Investors looking for market news and views on stocks and the markets.

Top Things to Do on This Site:
1. Check out what's being said about a particular stock on the BullBoards, or see which stocks are generating the most buzz.
2. Paying subscribers can use the MediaScan feature to find mentions of a company or stock in 600 global publications.

Toys:
1. A stock portfolio tracker.
2. E-mail alerts when stocks in your portfolio make the news. Note the "vacation mode" feature, which allows you to turn off the e-mail flow from StockHouse while you're away. A simple but brilliant idea. Everyone should copy this.

LINKS

Globeinvestor.com (www.globeinvestor.com): The king of Canadian investing Web sites, Globeinvestor offers a thorough database on North American-listed stocks, as well as news and investing stories from *The Globe and Mail* newspaper.

TheLion.com

What's the Deal?:
A search engine that gives you access to all major stock discussion forums on the Web.

Usefulness Rating: ✓✓✓✓✓

Canadian Content Rating: ✓✓

Cost: Free

Some of the top online stock discussion forums can be found on Silicon Investor, Raging Bull, Yahoo Finance, and Motley Fool. If you wanted to do a thorough survey of what investors were saying about a stock, you would probably want to take a look at all or most of these sites, and possibly others as well. There are two ways to do this, the first being to go to each site individually and then type in the symbol of your stock. The more sensible alternative is to use TheLion.com to find postings about your stock on all of the major discussion forums at once.

Say you're following Cisco Systems, the giant producer of telecommunications equipment, and you want to monitor what people are saying about it. With TheLion.com, you would type in the symbol CSCO and then let the Web site present you with a list of recent postings. When I tried a Cisco search, it was an hour or so before the company was set to make an eagerly anticipated quarterly earnings announcement. Using TheLion.com, I was able to track literally hundreds of postings on Silicon Investor, Raging Bull, Yahoo Finance, the Motley Fool, and CNBC. Postings were flying thick and fast, but TheLion.com funnelled them all in and presented them sequentially.

TheLion.com organizes its searches like most other online discussion forums. You get a quick preview of the message, the name of the person posting the message, and the date and time of the posting. Unlike the others, TheLion.com adds the source of the posting, i.e. the online message board where the posting originated. If you want to see which stocks are coming up most often on discussion forums during a given day, then scroll down TheLion.com's homepage for the so-called Stock Buzz Index.

Canadian Stocks on TheLion.com

High-visibility Canadian stocks listed on U.S. stock exchanges are covered fairly well in TheLion.com's database, but you can pretty much forget about finding anything significant for stocks that are listed only on the Toronto Stock Exchange. If you want to try anyway, type .TO after the ticker symbol, as in CP.TO. ∎

If you track a stock on TheLion.com, you'll find that the listing of messages is always preceded by a set of links that will allow you to do fairly thorough research on the company. A couple of the links stand out, including one under the title "Buzz Index" that will take you to a Web site called Validea (one of the 50 essential sites in this book), where you'll see what top pundits have said about your stock lately. The other link is to an online analysis service called Tradetrek (www.tradetrek.com) that will give you unique things like a six-month price prediction. The Lion.com also maintains a huge archive of links to outside investing Web sites—to find it, just click where it says "Research" on the homepage.

The Lion.com offers a few other neat features, including an "all-in-one post" that lets you send the same message to multiple discussion forums chosen by you. There's also a feature that allows you to either block or highlight a particular message board poster.

THELION.COM AT A GLANCE

Who's It For?
People who want a quick way of scanning what's being said on the major online discussion forums.

Top Things to Do on This Site
1. Check the buzz on a particular stock.
2. See which stocks are being talked about the most.
3. Use the better-than-average stock research tools.

Don't Miss:
Trading Lessons, a feature that offers investing tips and advice.

Toys
1. TheLion Navigator: Attaches to your regular Web browser's toolbar, adding buttons that allow you to do quick message searches and to access TheLion.com research tools.

LINKS

Raging Bull (www.ragingbull.com): A top online discussion forum.

Silicon Investor (www.siliconinvestor.com): One of the foremost online stock talk sites, Silicon Investor also offers a pretty decent set of stock research tools.

StockHouse (www.stockhouse.ca): The StockHouse BullBoards are a top forum for investors who want to talk about Canadian stocks.

Yahoo Finance (finance.yahoo.com): Popular message boards are part of the wide selection of investing tools on this site.

TheStreet.com

What's the Deal?:
Super-savvy commentary on the markets.

Usefulness Rating: ✓✓✓✓

Canadian Content Rating: ✓✓

Cost: An excellent basic service is free; a premium service called Real-Money.com costs $19.95 (U.S.) per month, or $199.95 per year.

If there's a more opinionated, fearless, credible, and amusing market commentator on the Web than James J. Cramer of TheStreet.com, I haven't read him or her. Here's Mr. Cramer, a one-time hedge fund manager, ranting about the incompetence of mutual fund managers who make big bets on a sector, score big, and then get whacked when the market falls: "Let's get personal for a second. These managers all hate me. You know why? Because I see the world through the eyes of a professional and I know they're a disgrace. They are full of excuses for their poor performance except for the most logical reason: 'I didn't know what I was doing.'"

Now, here's Mr. Cramer expounding on his view that rhetoric from fund managers about the need to focus on long-term performance is just a lame excuse for bad results: "Here's the problem with the long-term bar. It is just too low. It is too loose. It is too forgiving because 'long-term' is endless. If last year was bad, 'Wait till you see long-term.' When this year turns out to be bad again we hear, 'You aren't thinking long-term.' As I never tire of saying, some decisions are *wrong*! They are not early. They are not 'Don't worry, it will work out.' They are just WRONG."

I don't know about you, but I can't get enough of this stuff. Most online stock commentary ranges from wishy-washy to guardedly opinionated, but Mr. Cramer lets it fly. What makes him all the more devastating is his background as a hands-on money manager. In fact, he used to manage a hedge fund and at the same time write a trading diary for TheStreet.com. Now, alas, Mr. Cramer mainly writes on mutual funds for the site, while his stock commentary is reserved for TheStreet.com's pay service, RealMoney.com.

Independent Research

TheStreet.com prides itself on its independent, unbiased reporting and analysis. Here are some excerpts from the site's Conflicts and Disclosure Policy:

Editorial Staffers

To avoid any appearance that our reporting is driven by personal interest, TheStreet.com, Inc. does not permit any employees on its editorial staff to individually hold positions in individual stocks, though they are permitted to own stock in TheStreet.com, Inc. The restriction is, to our knowledge, among the most stringent in financial journalism.

Editorial staffers are permitted to own mutual funds. However, if a staffer writes about a mutual fund in which he or she holds shares, appropriate disclosure is made.

Outside Columnists

Outside contributing columnists for TheStreet.com and RealMoney.com... may from time to time write about stocks in which they or their firms have a position. In such cases, appropriate disclosure is made. ■

Don't get the idea that TheStreet.com revolves around Mr. Cramer. It doesn't, even though he's a co-founder and director of the site. There are actually about three dozen other columnists who contribute regularly, and a newsroom full of editors and journalists. Together, they produce dozens of stories each trading day that provide some of the most useful daily market commentary around.

If there's a problem with TheStreet.com, it's that there is almost too much available to users. A couple of times, I found an interesting column or investing tool and then was unable to locate it a second time without all kinds of clicking around the site. For this reason, I suggest you meander your way through the site to get a feel for it. Start by reading the day's top news headlines on the homepage, then click your way through the "Market," "Tech Stocks," and "Company News" areas. Then, try the "Insight & Advice" and "Managing Your Money" sections, where you'll find TheStreet.com's columnists, including Mr. Cramer. Eventually, you'll come to recognize the useful features on the site and be able to find them quickly. And—who knows?—maybe TheStreet.com will actually figure out a better way to guide users through its many features.

TheStreet.com is one of the earliest examples of that now rare species, the dotcom. On the day the company's shares began trading in May 1999, they rose from the $19 (U.S.) price of their initial public offering to close at $60. While the site's credibility and audience grew, profitability proved elusive. Layoffs ensued, a U.K. newsroom was closed, and at the time this was being written, the share price had fallen to the $1.25 range.

In this context, you'll understand why TheStreet.com is so eager to steer its audience to its main subscription-based service, RealMoney.com. RealMoney.com, which costs $19.95 (U.S.) per month or $199.95 per year, is aimed at active investors and market enthusiasts seeking more timely, harder-edged coverage than you'll find on TheStreet.com. Notable features are real-time stock quotes, Trading Track, which is described as a real-time e-journal of the thoughts and plays of investing professionals, and online chats with columnists. It used to be that material on RealMoney.com appeared on TheStreet.com after 24 hours, but this policy seems to have been modified to keep some features exclusive to RealMoney.com. NOTE: TheStreet.com offers a 30-day free trial of RealMoney.

Though its forte is market commentary, TheStreet.com broadens out its coverage by including a comprehensive stock research area that includes charting, analyst recommendations and earnings estimates, profiles, financials, and a list of relevant articles from TheStreet.com. There's also a set of online calculators related to investing in stocks—you'll find a link on the homepage under "Tools." In the past, TheStreet.com has also undertaken a massive effort to rank the work of brokerage analysts. Most such rankings on other Web sites look mainly at the ability of analysts to accurately forecast earnings and share prices, and how their recommendations pan out over time. TheStreet.com looked at these issues, but it also factored in the degree to which analysts are respected by institutional investors, which means heavy hitters like pension funds, insurance companies, banks, and so on.

THESTREET.COM AT A GLANCE

Who's It For?
Investors looking for smart, pointed commentary on the markets, stocks, and investing in general.

Top Things to Do on This Site:
1. Read the commentary by James J. Cramer and other columnists.
2. Keep up with the day's stock market news.
3. Try a free 30-day trial subscription to RealMoney.com

Don't Miss:
The "Second Opinion" feature, which you can access by using the tickerbox on the homepage for a quote. Provided by a service called Market Edge, Second Opinion will tell you whether to buy or avoid a stock based on technical indicators.

Toys:

1. Free e-mail bulletins: There's a twice-daily recap of market and company news, a personal finance newsletter called Managing Your Money, a tech stock newsletter, and a roundup of columns by James J. Cramer on mutual funds and other topics. You can receive these newsletters if you sign up for a free membership.

2. online financial calculators: A great collection of stock, mutual fund, bond, and financial planning calculators.

LINKS

Briefing.com (www.briefing.com): Similar to TheStreet.com in that it provides opinionated but unbiased market commentary. The presentation is a little rougher, and there's less variety in the stories available.

CBS MarketWatch (cbs.marketwatch.com): A glitzy, well-executed market news site that goes for a broader audience than TheStreet.com.

IDEAadvisor (www.ideaadvisor.com): Quick-hit analysis on the day's notable stocks. The emphasis is on providing guidance about whether a stock is a buy or not.

ThomsonFN.com

www.thomsonfn.com

What's the Deal?:
Stock analysis tools for the savvy, active investor.

Usefulness Rating: ✓✓✓✓

Canadian Content Rating: ✓✓

Cost: Free

ThomsonFN is a Web site for anyone who wants to look in on the trades that big institutional investors and corporate insiders are making. Follow their leads and you may just happen upon an investing opportunity that would otherwise have gone unnoticed, or you may avoid a trap. Intel Corp., the giant computer chipmaker, is a perfect example. While checking ThomsonFN's listing of unusual institutional activity one day, I found Intel mentioned as a stock with unusual buying activity.

Intel's been a market favourite for a long time, but the company had recently been weathering a rough period caused by a slowdown in demand for personal computers. The share price was off sharply and had shown only the most tepid signs of a turnaround. Using ThomsonFN, though, it became apparent that institutional investors—big pension funds, mutual funds, brokerage houses, and so on—had slowly but definitely warmed to the stock over the previous month. As bullish signs go, this one was pretty solid.

Now, what about the Intel senior executives who had access to non-public financial information about the company? Did these insiders see enough evidence of an improvement in the company's fortunes to start buying the stock? Uh, no. ThomsonFN's database of insider trades showed that there hadn't been much insider trading at all, but what there was appeared to be selling only. So what to make of Intel? Maybe the stock analysis area on ThomsonFN could help.

First, I called up a tipsheet that offered an overview of the stock, including the consensus analyst recommendation—a hold. There were also data showing Intel's share price momentum compared to the S&P 500 stock index—weak. Next, I did some charting to compare the trajectory of Intel's share price with insider trading patterns, an exercise that showed that when company insiders dumped shares it was a reliable sign of another down cycle for the stock. For the sake of a longer-term perspective, I also created a chart showing Intel's five-year performance versus both the Nasdaq and S&P 500. Despite its recent troubles, Intel had still outperformed both by a significant margin. The bottom line here seemed to be that Intel was a stock with a great past and an uncertain future. Let the institutional managers buy Intel, I concluded. I'll pass.

Free Real-Time Quotes

ThomsonFN is one of a small number of investing Web sites that gives away free real-time quotes. Sign-up is easy, if a little time-consuming in that you have to read through several long documents and click to show that you agree not to share the real-time data with any market professionals. Once you're signed up, just type a stock symbol into the tickerbox on the homepage and click your mouse in the designated spot to indicate you want a real-time quote. ∎

ThomsonFN is operated by Thomson Financial Solutions, a top provider of electronic data services to the financial industry and a part of Toronto-based Thomson Corp. ThomsonFN uses some of the high-powered tools as its parent company offers to big institutional investors, which means this is a site that will come across as being somewhat arcane for the average small investor looking for a few good blue chips to stuff in an RRSP. This isn't to say that less-savvy investors should steer clear of ThomsonFN. To the contrary, the site has some very good explanatory material to help you interpret the insider and institutional trading data it displays.

For example, let's take a look at the insider trading section on ThomsonFN, which you can find by clicking on the "Insider" button on the toolbar at the top of the homepage. Several Web sites can give you basic information on what corporate insiders are doing with their shares, including Yahoo Finance, which offers data on U.S. and some inter-listed Canadian stocks. Things are done a little differently on ThomsonFN. Instead of just listing the details of who's buying or selling, this site looks at the correlation between the buying and selling by specific insiders and moves in the share price. Scores are then applied to insiders based on the prescience of their buy and sell transactions. Top scorers can be considered the most adept at finding advantageous points to move in and out of a company's stock.

If an insider receives a score of 60 or more, it typically means her company's stock has either gone up in the six months after she bought shares, or fallen in the six months after she sold. The most reliable insiders—the so-called First Team All-Stars—have earned scores of 80 to 100. On average, these people have bought shares in their company and seen them rise an average 33.4 per cent within six months. On the flip side, the shares have fallen 27.2 per cent on average after they were sold. ThomsonFN says its all-stars represent about 14,000 of the 150,000 corporate insiders filing to U.S. securities authorities.

Insider Trading—It's Not What You Might Think

If all this talk about insiders conjures up images of dishonest insider trading, don't fret. Insiders legitimately buy and sell holdings in their companies all the time. It's only illegal when they trade on news about the company that the public doesn't know about.

An insider, by the way, is someone at a company who is exposed to key non-public financial information. ■

Each day, ThomsonFN offers lists of buy and sell transactions by people whose past trading patterns have earned them high scores. You'll also find lists of the Top 10 insider trades by market value, and the day's unusual insider events. This latter category is well worth checking regularly because it offers some particularly telling market intelligence. For example, there are listings of the largest-ever insider buy or sell transactions at a company, and the companies with insider buying while the stock is at a 52-week high. Executives who buy their own company's shares at a high point are showing a unique level of confidence in the future. There is also a tally of insiders dumping shares when they are at a 52-week low. Now there's a strong signal to avoid a stock.

One of the most appealing things about ThomsonFN's insider trading area is the many ways that the data are usefully sliced and diced. For instance, there's an "Ideas" area where you'll find handy lists that can help suggest stocks worthy of further research. I suggest taking a look at the list of companies where unusual insider trading patterns have occurred, perhaps indicating a shift in sentiment one way or another.

ThomsonFN is essentially a data site, which means it offers numbers and an explanation of how you can interpret them. For this reason, I think the site offers a good complement to commentary sites like TheStreet.com or Briefing.com. You might start with ThomsonFN, getting a sense of what insiders and institutions are doing on a given day and then switch over to a commentary site to see if the resident experts have keyed in on the same stocks. Conversely, you could pick up on a stock highlighted on one of the commentary sights and then run it through ThomsonFN's analytics.

THOMSONFN.COM AT A GLANCE

Who's It For?
Investors who want to look at institutional and insider trading patterns to help them choose stocks.

Top Things to Do on This Site:
1. Check out the day's notable institutional and insider buying and selling activity.
2. Check the notable buying and selling by corporate insiders.
3. Follow the day's hot and cold stocks and sectors.

Don't Miss:
ThomsonFN's stock research area. Click where it says "Stocks" at the top of the homepage and then work your way through the data. A highlight is the seasonality tracker, which provides information on month-by-month historical stock performance.

Toys:
1. Free real-time stock quotes.
2. E-mail alerts when insiders buy or sell at a company you're watching.
3. Wealth Tracker, a sophisticated portfolio-tracking tool.

LINKS

MSN Money (moneycentral.msn.com): This excellent investing site offers data on insider trading, and on which institutional investors are the biggest shareholders in a particular company.

Validea

What's the Deal?:

Rankings on how well media pundits do in their stock-picking, as well as a database on which stocks are being mentioned by the investing media.

Usefulness Rating: ✓✓✓✓✓

Canadian Content Rating: ✓✓

Cost: $14.95 per month (U.S.) or $149.95 per year; minimal free services

V alidea answers a question that all but the most sheep-like investors have asked at one point or another: Which financial writers, media personalities, and pundits are most worth paying attention to, and which should be ignored? Validea tracks the investment ideas contained in some 35 different sources in print, online, and on television. *Business Week*, *Forbes*, *Fortune* are included, as are MSN Money, CNBC.com, CNNfn TV, and Wall Street Week with Louis Rukeyser. In all, Validea claims to follow 6,500 different stock-pickers and 60,000 recent stock picks.

When I tried Validea for the first time, my first inclination was to check up on *Fortune* magazine, which I subscribed to at the time.

Fortune frequently offers stock suggestions, and they're usually big, brand-name companies. How had *Fortune's* picks worked out? To find out, I clicked on the "Sources" button on the homepage and then selected "Quick Stats" from the drop-down menu. I then typed Fortune into the search engine that popped up. Both *Fortune* and Fortune.com are listed—I chose the former. What I learned was that *Fortune's* stock picks had absolutely killed the Standard & Poor's 500 stock index over the previous year by a margin of 41 per cent to seven per cent.

Fortune's stock picks also shamed other investing publications. Three months after *Fortune* issued its suggestions, they were up 5.8 per cent, while the average publication's picks were up 2.6 per cent. After a year, *Fortune* was up 20.4 per cent and the average publication 3.9 per cent. Other nuggets included a list of recent *Fortune* picks, and a list of successes and duds from the past few years. The successful picks included Globix and Internet Capital Group, while the dud highlights were Amazon.com and Ariba.

I also learned on Validea that *Fortune* scored reasonably well against online and TV-based pundits based on the three-month performance of its stock picks. In fact, *Fortune* received a rating of four light bulbs out of five, good enough for sixth place. Among the sources that topped the magazine were a couple of Web sites you'll find in this book—Individual Investor and MSN Money.

If you want to get the most out of Validea, spend some time fooling around with its many features. On the homepage, you'll find links to a list of new stock picks, most-frequently-mentioned stocks (positively and negatively), and "guru-tested" stocks, which means stocks that have attracted strong or moderate interest from media gurus. A company called Gilead Sciences caught my eye on the most-mentioned list. That's because Gilead had been mentioned six times in the past week in the media sources tracked by Validea, with all mentions being positive. I clicked on Gilead's stock symbol and found that the stock had actually had a dozen positive mentions over the previous six months, with nary a discouraging word. As Validea showed, Gilead is a pharmaceutical company specializing in viral diseases. *Barron's* had run a positive story on the stock, as had CNBC, Bloomberg TV, MSN Money, and Worldly Investor, among others.

You've Got Mail from Validea

There's no way you can possibly keep track of what all the investing magazines, Web sites, and television shows are saying about particular stocks, so don't even try. Instead, let Validea tip you off each day about which stocks were mentioned by which source. All you do is sign up for Validea's daily Media Buzz Highlights e-mail service. At the top of each e-mail is a list of articles or write-ups and the sources where they appeared. If an article interests you, just click on the name of the source and you'll jump to its Web site for the complete story. If the article is on specific stocks, then you can also click on the name of the stock and be taken to a Validea page that lists all recent media mentions of the company. Note: Validea offered its e-mail for free at press time.

A sample e-mail I received included references to a write-up on Yahoo Inc. that appeared in RedHerring.com, a look at Abercrombie and Fitch on Smart Money.com, Worldy Investor's take on Dollar General, and a *Forbes* magazine analysis of top U.S. bank stocks.

Here's a sampling of the nuggets of information you get when you sign up for Validea's free "Spotlights of the Week" e-mail.

-Top experts and their latest picks: the latest picks from the experts with the best success over the previous three months.
-Most-mentioned stocks: the five stocks most often mentioned, in the sector talked about most in the past week.
-Guru-tested stocks: stocks that meet the criteria of a variety of different investing strategies. ■

Validea provided a quick recap of what each media source said about Gilead, and the information was quite informative. Worldly Investor pointed out that Gilead had six products on the market that were expected to generate revenue of $1-billion (U.S.), while MSN Money noted that the company was a pick of the editor of a respected biotech newsletter.

Validea is the work of John Reese, a high-tech entrepreneur who found himself wondering a few years ago which of the major investing magazines offered the best-performing stock recommendations. He then began keeping track of recommended stocks by monitoring their performance from the date they were first mentioned. Validea has improved a lot since it first appeared. Where once the experts were simply listed by name, now there's a bit of context to tell you what kind of stocks they're experts on. I noticed one day that online columnist Mitch Ratcliffe wasn't doing too well. It turned out that Mr. Ratcliffe talked mostly about technology stocks, which were being hammered at the time.

A worthwhile toy offered by Validea is the Guru Stock Screener (click where it says "Stocks" at the top of the homepage), which will find stocks that have received moderate and/or strong interest from two, three, four, or five gurus—your choice. Or you can screen stocks according to a number of different strategies, including those developed by Peter Lynch, the legendary one-time manager of Fidelity's Magellan Fund, and Benjamin Graham, the father of value investing.

You can also run searches by source, sector, and type of comment (positive or negative). Maybe you would like to know all the stocks panned by *Forbes* magazine. When I checked, a *Forbes* article had just come out with some negative comments about four U.S. banks. Or maybe you would like to know the ranking of online Validea sources over the previous 12 months. Individual Investor took top honours when I checked, followed by MSN Money. To me, one of the most useful Validea features is the list of most-mentioned stocks. You can set the search engine to include only top-rated sources (five lightbulbs), and you can customize the timeframe and stock sector.

Finally, you can simply take a stock that interests you and see what Validea digs up. I did this for Solectron, a U.S. contract electronics manufacturing stock that I bought a while ago. The result: Whew, vindicated. Though Solectron had come through a recent bad patch, the stock had received 28 positive mentions in the previous six months and just four negative ones. There was also a summary list of all the positive comments, with links to the full articles in which the comments appeared.

For Canadian investors, Validea should be viewed mainly, but not exclusively, as a source of information on U.S. stocks. A few predictable Canadian issues come up frequently in the Validea database, but there are some surprises as well. For example, I found four mentions of Canadian Pacific over the previous six months, including a favourable one by James J. Cramer, the feisty commentator who appears on TheStreet.com. My random checks also located five mentions of BCE and QLT, three of Toronto-Dominion Bank, and one each of TransCanada PipeLines, Cognos, and Corel. The Canadian stalwarts on Validea were companies such as Nortel Networks, with 146 mentions over the previous six months, and PMC Sierra, with 61 mentions.

The interesting thing about these mentions of Canadian companies is that they come from U.S. media sources. I'm not suggesting there's something thrilling about a Canadian stock being noticed by U.S. pundits, although this is generally rare. Rather, the U.S. perspective on stocks that are familiar to us can sometimes offer unique insights. I looked up the sole mention of TransCanada PipeLines mentioned earlier and was surprised to find it came from Jim Jubak, a columnist on MSN Money whose work I have enjoyed. Mr. Jubak had written an article in which he argued that energy stocks should no longer be viewed as a cyclical play, but rather as a way to capitalize on a long-term rise in demand for commodities such as natural gas. Mr. Jubak suggested TransCanada in particular because it was active in electrical power generation as well as pipelines. By the way, Validea gave Mr. Jubak a rating of three bulbs out of five.

VALIDEA AT A GLANCE:

Who's It For?
Investors who want to assess the reliability of their favourite sources of investing intelligence, as well as those who want to know what stocks top pundits are discussing.

Top Things to Do on This Site:
1. Check the quality of the investing publications and Web sites you commonly use.
2. See what experts have to say about stocks you're following.
3. Troll for investing ideas by seeing what the experts are talking about.

Don't Miss:

The "Most Mentioned" feature—there's no better way to tell which stocks are generating the most buzz at the moment. You'll find it under "Stocks" on the homepage.

Toys:

1. Daily Media Buzz e-mails that list the top investing articles of the day.

2. Nightly portfolio updates that let you know if one of your stocks was mentioned in the investing media.

3. Portfolio tracking that enables you to run your portfolio through the Validea database so you can see what the experts are saying about what you own.